Making an Impact

RANDALL J. BREWER

CONTENTS

INTRODUCTION 1

1 "GREATER THAN YOU THINK" 4

2 "EXAMPLES TO FOLLOW" 16

3 "MAXIMIZE YOUR LIFE" 27

4 "A LIFE LIVED WELL" 40

5 "CITY ON A HILL" 51

6 "COMMON GROUND" 63

7 "A BETTER PLACE" 74

8 "SEEDS OF BLESSING" 85

9 "A LEGACY OF GENEROSITY" 97

10 "A GIFT FROM GOD" 109

11 "APPLE OF HIS EYE" 120

IV –

12 "REDEEMING THE TIME" 131

13 "A FOUNTAIN OF LIFE" 142

14 "NEW FRONTIERS" 154

15 "NO GREATER JOY" 165

16 "MARCHING ORDERS" 178

SUMMARY 189

MAKING AN IMPACT

INTRODUCTION

We live in a world desperate for light, for hope, and for people willing to make a difference. Every day, the headlines remind us of the darkness that covers the earth-violence, greed, corruption, and despair. Yet, in the midst of it all, God still calls His people to be salt and light, to shine brightly and influence the world for His glory. This book, "Making an Impact," is a call to rise above the noise of the age and step boldly into the purpose for which you were created—to make an eternal impact wherever God has placed you.

The truth is, God never intended for His children to live ordinary, self-focused lives. From the very beginning, He commanded His people to "be fruitful and multiply, and fill the earth" (Genesis 1:28). This was not only a call to reproduce physically, but spiritually - to fill the earth with His image, His love, and His truth. Every believer carries within them the divine potential to shape culture, influence people, and change the atmosphere around them through the power of Christ.

But making an impact doesn't always mean standing on a stage, leading a movement, or reaching millions. Sometimes it's the quiet acts of faithfulness that change the world most profoundly - a kind word to a stranger, a prayer offered in secret, an honest deed when no one else is watching. True impact begins in the heart that says, "Lord, use me." It begins with a life surrendered to God's will, a life that reflects His nature in every sphere of influence - at home, at work, in the community, and in the church.

Jesus Himself lived this example. Though He never wrote a book or held a political office, His influence has transformed nations and shaped history for over two thousand years. He invested in people. He healed the sick, fed the hungry, spoke truth with love, and embodied compassion everywhere He went. And when He called His disciples, He told them, "Follow Me, and I will make you fishers of men." In other words, He would transform their lives so that through them, others might be transformed as well. That is the essence of impact - being changed so that others can be changed through you.

In today's world, it's easy to feel small, to think that one life cannot possibly make a difference amidst the enormity of global issues. But history is filled with stories of individuals who dared to believe otherwise - men and women who allowed God to use them despite their limitations. Noah built an ark in obedience and saved humanity. Esther risked her life to save her people. Daniel remained faithful in Babylon and influenced kings. Each of them proved that one person fully surrendered to God can leave a mark that lasts for generations.

Making an impact, then, is not about striving for fame or recognition; it's about obedience. It's about letting your light shine so that others may see your good works and glorify your Father in heaven (Matthew 5:16). It's about aligning your daily actions with eternal purpose, knowing that even the smallest seed of kindness, faith, or truth can bear fruit beyond what you can see.

This book will challenge you to examine your influence, to ask how your life reflects the Kingdom of God in a world that desperately needs to see it. It will help you understand that your presence on this earth is not accidental. You were born for such a time as this. You are called to be a difference-maker in your family, your workplace, your church, and your community.

In the chapters ahead, we will explore what it truly means to make an impact that lasts - how to live with intentionality, serve with humility, and love with the compassion of Christ. We will look at biblical principles that empower believers to stand firm in truth, to operate in God's power, and to leave a legacy that points others to Him.

Your life is meant to count for something greater than yourself. Heaven is watching, the world is waiting, and the time is now. God has placed within you everything you need to make an impact. The question is, will you answer the call?

| 1 |

"GREATER THAN YOU THINK"

God is a supernatural God and He wants to do the supernatural through you. In other words, He wants you to make an impact on your generation. He wants your influence to reach into the darkest corners of this planet. He wants you to boldly go where no man has gone before. God is speaking to you all the time telling you what His purpose for your life is. Listen to Him. Lean into Him and hear what He's saying to your heart. Powerful things happen when you hear His voice and say you'll do what He tells you to do, when you say what Isaiah said, "Here I am! Send me" (Is. 6:8). There was a need and Isaiah responded with no hesitation. Isaiah was in the presence of God and for him there was no other response to give. God did not lay a strong compulsion on Isaiah. He didn't come with pressure and pleadings. He just stated a need and Isaiah responded accordingly. Isaiah gave his life in service to God because he wanted to impact the world he lived in. He offered himself as a blank check to be filled as God saw fit.

God is a big God and He wants to do big things through you. He wants to use you to do the impossible. He wants to use you to change the world you live in. Rejoice and be highly encouraged knowing that your usefulness in God's kingdom has the potential for eternal impact. Let God direct your steps, and you'll soon realize that your influence in this dark world will be greater than you think. The God you serve is not limited by human boundaries, natural laws, or earthly expectations. He is the God who parts seas, calms storms, heals the broken, restores the ruined, and brings life where death once reigned. Nothing about Him is ordinary. Nothing about His power is restrained. He is the supernatural God, and He delights in revealing His greatness through those who believe. What many people fail to realize is God does not simply do the supernatural around you - He desires to do it through you. You were never called to live a powerless life. You were created to be a vessel, a carrier of His glory, a living demonstration of His strength on the earth.

The same Spirit that raised Jesus from the dead lives in you, energizing your faith, empowering your prayers, and equipping your steps. God is looking for people who will dare to believe Him - people who will step beyond the natural, trust beyond what they see, and act on the impossible word He puts in their hearts. When you live with an expectation of the supernatural, heaven responds. Miracles begin to flow. Doors open. Provision comes. Healing manifests. Lives are changed. You are not ordinary because the God inside you is not ordinary. You are not weak because the Spirit within you is not weak. You are not limited because the One who called you has no limits. Today, lift your faith. Raise your expectations. Position your heart to be used by the God who delights in doing the impossible. Let Him work through you. Let Him speak through you. Let Him display His power through your surrendered life. The world is waiting to see what God can do through someone who simply believes. Let that person be you.

Booker T. Washington once said, "There is no person on earth that can neutralize the influence of a high, simple, and useful life." God has called you to look beyond yourself to the impact you can have on those who cross your path. Talk to people and pass on to them your values, lessons learned from successes and defeats. Tell them about the essence of your life. Pour your energy into a renewed effort to capitalize on all the wisdom you've learned over the years to broaden your influence in the world. You will cross paths with many people during your lifetime, and you'll make an impact on their lives by passing on to them your knowledge and wisdom. When you talk to people ignite a fire in them as you guide them into a love for Jesus Christ. Repeatedly give them your time and wisdom. Share with others the lessons you've learned about life, about faith, about relationship. Do this and you'll make the world a better place.

Your calling in life is to help people become smarter, better balanced, and more effective in their life. Cheer them on as you impart to them the courage to persevere. Your legacy involves influencing others to walk the straight and narrow. Believe in these people and show them what they're capable of. People desperately need to feel the heat of a life on fire for God. In a world growing colder by the day - cold in love, cold in mercy, cold in conviction - God is searching for men and women who burn with holy passion. The greatest testimony is not always a sermon or a song; often it is simply the sight of a life that radiates the warmth of God's presence. When a person is truly on fire for God, others can feel it. Their fire ignites courage, awakens hope, and melts hardened hearts. It draws the broken, the weary, and the lost - not because of who you are, but because of Who burns within you. A candle without flame cannot light another; but one burning brightly can set a whole room ablaze.

Let your passion become a spark that awakens something deep within other people. Create in them the desire to know the God who still consumes, still purifies, still empowers. So fan the flame. Guard it. Feed it. Live close enough to God that His fire becomes your fire. Let your worship be bold, your obedience unwavering, your love undeniable. Why? Because somewhere nearby, someone cold in spirit is reaching for warmth. Someone stumbling in darkness is looking for light. Someone surrounded by despair is searching for heat. Let your life burn so brightly that they can feel it. Let them see what a life on fire for God really looks like and let that fire spread. A person on fire for God knows the way, shows the way, and goes the way. There is no better influence than a good example. Godly influence doesn't begin with the spiritual gifts and abilities you have. It begins with the direction your life is going.

Paul said it best in 1 Cor. 11:1 (CEV), "You must follow my example, as I follow the example of Christ." AMP, "Pattern yourselves after me. Follow my example." There is a beautiful simplicity in Paul's words. In one sentence, Paul captures the heart of true discipleship. He is not pointing people to himself; he is pointing them through himself to Jesus. Paul understood that a life surrendered to Christ becomes a living testimony. Your attitude, choices, and behavior preach louder than your voice ever could. When you follow Christ sincerely, consistently, and wholeheartedly, your life becomes an invitation for others to encounter Him. Paul wasn't claiming to be perfect. He was simply saying, "Look at the direction I'm going. I'm pursuing Christ with everything in me. Walk with me as I walk with Him." This is the call for every believer. To live in such a way that others can safely follow our footsteps because our footsteps are following Jesus.

If you're following Christ, you're going in the right direction. You're making an impact when you take others with you. Paul also said in Phil. 3:17, "Brethren, join in following my example and observe those who walk according to the pattern you have in us." Going in the right direction enables you to imitate Christ in all your sphere of influence as you seek to bring glory and honor to the King of kings and Lord of lords. Writing to the saints at Corinth Paul said, "Therefore I urge you, imitate me" (1 Cor. 4:16). Live your life in such a way that you can say the same thing. Let your life be a reflection of Christ's character, His humility, His courage, His compassion, and His holiness. Let your choices reflect His love. Let your actions speak of His grace. And let your walk inspire others to take steps of faith. May your life say to those around you, "Follow me, as I follow Him." There is no higher calling than to let your life mirror the character of Jesus Christ. Your life is meant to shine with His presence, not just in words, but in attitude, conduct, and love.

An imitator is one who follows. The Greek word "mimetes" means 'to copy or imitate someone's behavior.' Webster's dictionary says the word "imitate" means 'to follow as a pattern, model, or example; to be or appear like.' Joyfully following Jesus and His divine direction will make you an example that others can imitate and follow when trials come their way. Imitate Christ. Let your actions speak louder than your words. Do that and you'll have a platform on which to make an impact on others. Take time and consider your sphere of influence. Know with certainty that God has placed you in the center of a circle of influence. All around you are people who need your influence in their life. They need you to make an impact on whatever it is they're going through. To make a positive difference in people's lives, you must be there when they need you. Make yourself available whether it's convenient for you or not. Just think, by spending some quality time with a hurting individual you may help save their marriage, their job, and even their life.

Life is a journey, and you can help take people to places they wouldn't go themselves. Pour into them life lessons that will take them to a higher level in life. There comes a time in every believer's journey when God calls you to pour into others what He has poured into you. Your experiences, your victories, your wisdom, and even your painful lessons were never meant to be kept in silence. They are seeds - divine deposits - given so you can plant them in the lives of others and help them grow into who God destined them to be. And, by all means, be purposeful and authentic. A phony can be spotted a mile away. Be honest and tell people the times you missed the mark and how Jesus rescued you in due time. Know with certainty that your influence matters. Never make light of the impact you can have in this generation and the generations to come. Theologian Henry Varley once said, "The world has yet to see what God can do with and for and through and in a man who is fully and wholly consecrated to Him." A man heard these words, closed his eyes and said, "I want to be that man." That man's name was D. L. Moody, one of the greatest evangelists of all time.

To influence others, you must first become the message you hope to share. In other words, you must live a godly life. Why? Because your character is the foundation your destiny is built on. True influence does not come from loud words or impressive displays—it flows from a life aligned with God. People are drawn to authenticity. They may hear what you say, but they are changed by how you live your life. When your character reflects Christ - your patience, your humility, your generosity, your integrity - your life becomes a light that others cannot ignore. Godly influence is not forced; it's revealed through daily obedience, quiet faithfulness, and consistent love. You influence others most powerfully when your lifestyle preaches the sermon your lips could never fully express. So walk with God. Let His Spirit shape your actions, purify your motives, and transform your heart. As you live a godly life, those around you will feel the pull of God's presence—and many will rise to follow the example they see in you. Live the life, and your life will lead others to Him.

It is important to know that your destiny will never grow beyond your character. You can't make a positive impact on others if you don't walk the straight and narrow. It is your calling and responsibility to let God produce in your life those godly qualities that others can see and imitate. God is a builder (Heb. 11:10) and He wants to build character in your life. This will take some time for we all know Rome was not built in a day. You will go through seasons where God will build in you one character trait and then another and then another one after that. It's a growing process. Is. 28:10 says, "Precept upon precept, line upon line, here a little, there a little." This means you'll grow progressively over a period of time. Spiritual growth is not an instant transformation - it is a journey built step by step, truth by truth. Every small lesson, every quiet insight, every moment of obedience is a building block in our understanding and our faith. In other words, you must be in this for the long haul. Commitment and perseverance will be forever needed on this journey to create in your godly character.

To be effective in ministry, in making an impact, it is important from time to time to consider your present position in life. Where are you in your spiritual journey? Have a serious review and assessment of where you are in your relationship with God. Are you praying in faith? Are you serving with zeal? Are you walking in humility? Are you worshipping with joy? Are you giving with gladness? Are you reaching out with love? Not only is God a builder, but He is also a patient builder. Building good things takes time. Anything built too quickly will have flaws, defects, and weaknesses. God often takes His time in doing things. He told the children of Israel, "And the Lord your God will drive out those nations before you little by little" (Deut. 7:22). David didn't kill Goliath until he first grew in confidence and reliance on God by first killing the lion and the bear. Even Jesus couldn't begin His ministry until He first "grew in wisdom and stature, and in favor with God and man" (Luke 2:52).

When things aren't going as fast as you'd like, take comfort knowing that God is a wise builder. Yes, He knows what He's doing. The Greek word for "wisdom" is "sophia" and is 'the ability to judge correctly and to follow the best course of action, based on knowledge and understanding.' God knows you better than you know yourself. He knows what you can handle and what you can't. When things aren't moving as quickly as you hoped, remember that God is a master builder who takes His time to produce a quality product. A builder who rushes creates structures that crumble. But a wise builder lays foundations deep enough to hold the weight of the future He's preparing for you. What feels like a pause is often God reinforcing your faith, strengthening your character, and aligning your path with His perfect plan. So take comfort. Even when you don't see the construction taking place, heaven is working behind the scenes. God is not confused. He is not late. He is not uncertain. He is building something solid, beautiful, and enduring in your life.

People of influence must have character. Why? Because character attracts loyalty. People won't follow you if they don't trust you. What is character? It's a commitment to a set of values without compromise. It's the dedication to a set of standards without wavering. A person with high standards exhibits character and class. They don't compromise their values and beliefs. They stay true to who they are. A person with character does not live by what's popular with the world, they live according to God's values, laws, and principles. Character speaks of the unimpaired state of one's mind and heart, of moral soundness and purity, of incorruptness, uprightness, and honesty. Your character determines the outcome of your life and your effectiveness in the kingdom of God. It's the gauge that tells how much influence you will have. If you want to be used by God, then you must possess a strong character. You must do what's right because it is right. The level of your character determines the level of your success and influence in the world.

Your influence in the world depends on your character and not your charisma and your talents. Charisma may draw attention, and talent may open doors, but only character keeps those doors open. True influence is not built on how loudly you speak, how gifted you appear, or how impressive your abilities may seem. It is built on the quiet strength of integrity, humility, and a heart that consistently reflects Christ. When you walk in integrity, people may not always applaud you, but they will trust you. When you walk in humility, you may not stand out to man, but you stand tall before God. When you walk in love, you leave behind more than memories - you leave an imprint on hearts. The world is full of talented voices, but God is raising up people of strong character - men and women who will influence others not because they shine the brightest, but because their light is genuine, steady, and pure. Focus on becoming the kind of person God can trust. Let Him shape your character. Let Him refine your heart.

A person's character is the sum of their temperament, thoughts, intentions, desires, and actions. A person of character locks themselves in the prison of their own convictions and throws away the key. Having character is when you put constant effort into causing your words and actions to work together as one. A person without character will say one thing, do another, and promise something else. Their words and actions are not integrated together. Character is based on those godly principles you hold dear on the inside and what people see on the outside. People of character are known for their honesty, ethics, and charity. Their lives are distinguished by persistent moral virtue. Character means to have integrity. It means to be one with yourself. The root word for "holiness" in the Hebrew language is "integrity." The foundation of trust is integrity. It means "to be one." It means your life is whole and your heart is not divided. Character in a man of God is a constant manifestation of Jesus in his life.

Gen. 1:26 says God made man in His image and then gave him dominion over all the earth. Notice that image came before dominion. The first thing God gave man was His image which translates into character. He knew that character was necessary before dominion was given. What this means is that character is more important than power. Power and dominion will kill you if you don't have the character to control it. God created you in His image and you've been given the mandate to influence the world with His character. We develop character by controlling our thoughts (Phil. 4:8), practicing Christian virtues (2 Peter 1:5,6), guarding our hearts (Prov. 4:22), and keeping good company (1 Cor. 15:33). Titus 2:7,8 (ESV), "Show yourself in all respects to be a model of good works, and in your teaching show integrity, dignity, and sound speech that cannot be condemned." As the excellence of gold is its purity and the excellence of art is its beauty, so the excellence of man is his character. Billy Graham said, "A chain is only as strong as its weakest link, and so it is with our character."

| 2 |

"EXAMPLES TO FOLLOW"

The lives of many people who influenced the world they lived in grace the pages of the Bible, in both the Old and New Testament. Go to God and pray that their strengths would find greater expression in your life, that you'll be able to make a positive impact like they did. Pray, "Lord, help me to be like David." David was the greatest king in the history of Israel. He was competent, courageous, committed, and confrontational. David was not perfect, but he possessed something God treasures more than flawless behavior - a heart fully turned toward Him. When we look at David's life, we see the pattern every believer should pursue. David loved God deeply, trusted God boldly, and worshiped God freely. He repented sincerely and obeyed God wholeheartedly. His greatest strength was his faith-based optimism. This gave him the courage to step up in challenging situations without hesitation. His faith in God moved him to attempt feats for God that most leaders would never have considered.

David believed so deeply in the power of God that a giant could not intimidate him and a murderous king could not paralyze him. Whatever enemy David faced he didn't rely on his own strength, he relied on the God who never fails. He endured rejection, betrayal, hardship, and delay, yet he kept his confidence in the Lord. He made mistakes, but he ran *to* God, not away from Him. And through it all, he maintained a spirit of worship, humility, and courage. With confidence David marched in whatever direction God pointed him, fully expecting grace and power to be revealed along the way. Those who desire to be like David expect to experience God's greatness and love, even when they're facing bleak circumstances. People today need to see that kind of faith and optimism. You can influence these people by leading them into the same confidence in God that you have. Pray and ask God to make you like David, to be a person who inspires hope in people no matter what it is they're going through.

Pray, "Lord, help me to be like Jonathan." He was David's closest friend, and his name means 'gift of God' or 'God has given.' Jonathan was a very bright and gifted young man and is one of Scripture's quiet giants, one whose greatness wasn't built on a throne, but on character. He reminds us that true spiritual maturity isn't measured by position, applause, or visibility, but by the depth of our loyalty, love, and trust in God. 1 Sam. 18:1 says, "Jonathan became one in spirit with David, and he loved him as himself." This love makes Jonathan one of the most admired people in the Bible. He stood by David when everyone else walked away. He supported God's plan even when it cost him personally. He celebrated another man's anointing, even though he was the natural heir to the throne. In a world full of envy, ambition, and comparison, Jonathan shows us the beauty of a heart free from jealousy - one that rejoices in what God is doing, even when it's not through us.

Jonathan loved David and never sacrificed his relationship with him to protect his own future. On the contrary, he put his heart on a platter and offered it to David. He gave David his royal robe, his armor, his bow, and his belt symbolically laying down his own future to honor God's. He chose obedience over opportunity, surrender over self-promotion, humility over entitlement. Jonathan's submission to the will of God caused him to give David his love and loyalty. He went a great length to protect David from his father who wanted to kill him. Be like Jonathan. Honor other people above yourself (Rom. 12:10), love them the same way Christ loves you (John 15:12,13). Use this love to help make the lives of other people better. Give them pleasant, sincere advice, seeking their highest good (Prov. 29:9). Challenge these people to press in and reach their full potential (Prov. 27:17). If you want to make an impact in the world, learn to love people the way Jonathan loved David. What better influence is there?

Pray, "Lord, help me to be like Joseph." Every believer is called to grow into the fullness of Christ, and one of the clearest examples of godly character in Scripture is Joseph, son of Jacob. His life shines as a testimony of faith, integrity, and steadfast trust in the Lord no matter the circumstance. He was a man of integrity, self-control, compassion, and he had a sense of purpose. Integrity is the unwavering determination in the heart to do right no matter what. Integrity is not just what people see, it's what you are. Integrity is consistently living with good character. It means you're honest, faithful, reliable, moral. It's what causes you to persevere in hard times (Ps. 25:21). Joseph's integrity and personal holiness left him uncorrupted by power and help him avoid political scandal, financial impropriety, and sexual seduction. He was able to influence people because he was always righteous and faithful. He remained unstained by the world until the end of his life.

Joseph held on to his integrity even when tempted to sin. Job said it best, "Till I die I will not remove my integrity from me. My righteousness I hold fast and will not let it go; My heart shall not reproach me as long as I live" (Job 27:5,6). Moral soundness and integrity come from a heart that is completely surrendered to God, from an unsoiled mind and a clear conscience. Joseph made a powerful impact in the world he lived in because his concern for others was exceeded only by his love and obedience to God. When you have integrity, when you have the quality of being complete and undivided, people will trust you and have faith in your judgment. So let every believer strive to be like Joseph, to be faithful in hardship, pure in temptation, hopeful in uncertainty, forgiving in victory, trusting in God at all times. May Joseph's life encourage you to rise higher, walk straighter, and shine brighter for the glory of God, reflecting the compassion of God even toward those who did you wrong.

Pray, "Lord, help me to be like Joshua." Ask Him to give you Joshua's decisiveness, for the ability to make decisions quickly and confidently. Being decisive means you don't take forever to make up your mind. Your convictions are based on the Word of God, and you stick with your chosen course of action. Decisiveness is having the power or quality of deciding, possessing determination, and being outright unmistakable. It is an excellent quality to possess. Joshua's finest moment was when he stood in front of the people and said, "Choose this day whom you will serve. As for me and my house, we will serve the Lord" (Josh. 24:15). A decisive man walks with clarity and unwavering faith. He knows the path God has set before him and refuses to be paralyzed by doubt or indecision. With absolute certainty about the major matters of life - choices of character, purpose, and integrity - he moves boldly, making decisions that align with God's truth.

Decisiveness based on the will of God is what makes you confident, intelligent, and strong. It is the key to effectively executing plans and achieving goals. A decisive person is confident in their decision-making abilities and is willing to commit to their choices even when faced with uncertainties and risks. God wants you to make wise decisions and has given you an open invitation to ask for wisdom (James 1:5). Trust the Lord and believe He'll give you the wisdom you need. A decisive man has absolute certainty regarding major life issues and makes right choices accordingly. They then influence others to make them as well. His decisiveness is not just for himself; it becomes a beacon for others. The journey of life is not to be taken lightly. The issues around which our lives revolve are eternal and worthy of bold decisions. People have to choose to follow God. You make an impact on the world by encouraging them to make bold decisions based on God-given direction.

Pray, "Lord, help me to be like Esther." Esther's life is a powerful example of courage, faith, and purpose. Though she lived in uncertain times and faced great risk, she chose to step into her God-given role with wisdom and boldness. An evil man by the name of Haman devised a plan to kill all the Jews in the empire and Esther found herself at the crossroads of her people's destiny. She was asked by her older cousin Mordecai to risk her life by pleading her people's case before her husband who was a dangerous king. She said, "I will do the right thing and if I perish, I perish." She was willing to lose her status as queen, and even her life, to do what God called her to do. Her courage wasn't a manifestation of reckless insanity. She simply believed that certain values were worth living and, if need be, dying for. Esther risked her life in order to save her people. Her faithfulness in the face of danger influenced the king to stop the evil scheme of Haman. Esther's courage should be an inspiration to all of us.

Her story reminds us that even in the face of great adversity, it is always possible to triumph. As queen, Esther used her position to bless her people, putting the needs of others before her own and recognizing her dependence on the Lord. People around the world need the children of God to step up and manifest the courage of Esther, to say to the evil on the earth, "Enough is enough." You'll make an impact on this world when you have the courage to do the right thing, even at the risk of losing your reputation, your status, your security, and even your life. Let us all strive to be like Esther, to be bold in faith, steadfast in prayer, and fearless in obedience. May we rise in our own "palaces" and speak for what is just, trusting that God has positioned us for a purpose far greater than ourselves. Like Esther, we are called to stand for righteousness, even when fear tempts us to stay silent. Very few people have the courage Esther had, and you need to ask God to let you be one of them.

Pray, "Lord, help me to be like Solomon." King Solomon, renowned for his wisdom, wealth, and discernment, serves as a timeless example for how we can live faithfully before God. His story reminds us that true greatness comes not from riches or power, but from seeking God's guidance in every decision. He was the wisest man who ever lived, and you should pray that you will have the wisdom to discern God's will in every situation. God promised Solomon anything he asked for and he chose an understanding heart. He wanted wisdom so he could influence the people by making good decisions on their behalf. Solomon was sober-minded and approached the Lord as a humble, obedient servant. He was rewarded for his meekness when God granted his request. Solomon is described as a man to whom God gave "wisdom and understanding beyond measure (1 Kings 4:29). He wrote 3000 proverbs and 1005 songs. No other person was ever given a greater gift of wisdom.

People stood in awe of Solomon because they perceived that the wisdom of God was in him. He made a powerful impact on the world, and the Bible depicts Solomon's reign as an era of unprecedented prosperity due to his divine wisdom. Pray for wisdom so you can bring a spiritual perspective to daily life. Prov. 16:16, "How much better to get wisdom than gold, to get insight rather than silver." Solomon received godly wisdom when he asked for it. You also can ask for wisdom. James 1:5, "If any of you lack wisdom, let him ask of God and it will be given to him." Once you receive this wisdom, use it to bless and influence others. Wisdom and discernment will help you understand the right type of help people need at any given time. Wisdom will give you penetrating intellect, insight, and perception. With God's help you'll have the capacity to make right judgments concerning His people. Let us pursue wisdom, embrace discernment, and walk humbly with our God.

Pray, "Lord, help me to be like Jeremiah." Called "the weeping prophet" because his heart was so tender, his emotional authenticity is something we should all pray for. Jeremiah's heart grieved over the sin and suffering of his people. During hard times Jeremiah didn't put on a game face pretending all was well. No, with rare honesty he expressed his true feelings to God. When the enemy seemed to be getting the upper hand, he admitted he felt abandoned and fearful of the future. He then let God restore his broken heart. Jeremiah was able to go from despair to hope when in the midst of disappointment, he opened his heart to divine strength and encouragement. He never lost confidence in the faithfulness of God. He wrote in Lam. 3;22,23, "For Your compassions never fail. They are new every morning; great is Your faithfulness." Following his example, we are called to intercede for others, carry the burdens of those around us, and pray earnestly for the lost and hurting.

When other people are hurting, go to them and help them spill out the truth of their broken hearts to God believing He will touch them in a special way. Don't pretend everything is okay when it's not. Weep with those who weep (Rom. 12:15). Few things bond people together like that of a common sorrow. A heartfelt tear can show more love than a million words. It is when you identify with their hurt and pain that they'll be open to your comfort and edification. The bond of tears is the strongest bond of all. Genuinely care when people are hurting. To influence hurting people, you must first have the same hurt feelings they have. Christian fellowship is more than just a pat on the back. It means sharing the burdens of others so that we all grow together and glorify the Lord. Being like Jeremiah does not mean living without struggle - it means allowing God to use our voices, our hearts, and even our tears for His purpose.

Pray, "Lord, help me to be like Peter." He was one of Jesus' closest disciples and was far from perfect. He was impulsive, outspoken, and sometimes fearful - but he was also courageous, passionate, and unwaveringly devoted to Christ. His life reminds us that God doesn't call the perfect; He calls the willing. Yes, Peter was reckless, headstrong, and self-assertive, but he was also quick to commit when action was to be taken. He was the first to publicly identify Jesus as the long-awaited Messiah. He took the initiative in honoring the Lord with that title. He was the only disciple to get out of the boat and walk on water toward Jesus and he was one of the first two disciples to witness the empty tomb. Peter shows all of us how important it is to take the initiative when something needs to be done before being asked to do it. People who take the initiative demonstrate they can think for themselves and take action when necessary. They have the drive to achieve and succeed.

Initiative is all about taking charge. It's a personal quality that shows a willingness to take responsibility and get things done. These are the people who make things happen. They see a problem and act on it. They don't just sit passively by and wait for opportunities to come. Followers of Christ who take the initiative don't sit and watch, they get up and take action to do and accomplish what God wants to be done. When someone has a need don't wait for them to ask for help. Take the initiative and offer them your support and assistance. You'll make an impact on other people by stepping forward and helping them find solutions to the problems they are facing. You'll influence them by your generosity. Being like Peter isn't about being flawless - it's about being faithful, repentant, and bold in following Christ. Let us embrace our weaknesses, rely on God's strength, and live a life marked by courage, devotion, and unwavering faith, just as Peter did.

Pray, "Lord, help me to be like Paul." His life reminds us that true discipleship is not measured by comfort, success, or popularity, but by unwavering devotion to God, courage in the face of trials, and a heart that longs to see others come to Christ. His unbelievable intensity to do the will of God no matter what the circumstances is something we should all desire. It was Paul who said, "Never be lazy, but work hard and serve the Lord enthusiastically" (Rom. 12:11 NLT). Can you feel the intensity in those words? He's saying to be fervent in spirit, to maintain the spiritual glow, to have a burning zeal to do the will of God no matter where it may take you. Your service to others should be an open display of passionate intensity. Be very sincere and show great enthusiasm about what you're doing in and for the kingdom. Through extreme intensity you'll have the spiritual power to influence other people. You'll be able to lift them up to a higher level in life.

Be like Paul who said, "I will gladly spend and be completely spent for the sake of the church" (2 Cor. 12:15). Paul endured hardships, persecution, and rejection, yet he remained steadfast, guided by the Spirit and empowered by God's grace. He did not conform to the ways of the world but instead allowed Christ to transform him completely. His life was marked by humility, love, and a tireless commitment to spreading the gospel. He said, "For me to live is Christ, to die is gain" (Phil. 1:21). "In a race there is only one winner. When I run a race, I do so to win" (1 Cor. 9:24). God is a "consuming fire" (Deut. 4:24) and He wants you to have the same intensity in your service to others. It's intensity that pulls you out of the slumber of doing nothing. The martyred missionary Jim Elliot wrote in his diary, "Wherever you are, be all there. Live to the hilt every situation you believe to be the will of God." Making an impact in this world should make your spirit boil. Be white hot as you bear one another's burdens (Gal. 6:2) and help them succeed in life.

| 3 |

"MAXIMIZE YOUR LIFE"

God created each of us with a divine purpose: to leave a positive and lasting impact on the lives of those around us. Every word we speak, every act of kindness we offer, and every moment we choose love over indifference carries eternal significance. Your influence isn't measured by fame or wealth but by the way you encourage, uplift, and inspire others to grow in faith and hope. When you live intentionally for God, your actions ripple outward, touching hearts you may never meet, planting seeds of goodness that can transform generations. Making a difference is not optional, it is the calling God has placed within each of us. Let your life be a reflection of His love, and you will fulfill His purpose, leaving a legacy that echoes far beyond your own days. God expects you to have a strong influence in somebody's life for good and it is your responsibility to make sure that happens. Don't get so caught up in your own wants and desires that you forget you have a mission from God to impact the world around you.

The power of your impact is going to be determined by the character of your life. God expects you to live a different kind of life than the world lives. Being different means choosing integrity when others compromise, showing kindness when others are harsh, and standing for truth when others remain silent. It means valuing humility over recognition, service over self-interest, and eternal rewards over temporary pleasures. 2 Cor. 6:17 says, "Come out from among them and be separate, says the Lord." This means you must live a pure, holy life. Rom. 12:2 says, "Stop being conformed to the likeness of the world and be transformed." Paul is saying to be different from everybody else. Why be different? Because it's being different that attracts people to you. This is how and when you can make an impact on their lives. Let us embrace this distinction, remembering that our ultimate example is Jesus Christ. In every decision, every word, and every action, let us reflect Him.

Jesus said in the sermon on the mount that you are the salt of the earth and the light of the world, like a city on a hill that cannot be hidden (Matt. 5:13,14). God has placed each of us on this earth not just to exist, but to season the world with joy, love, and light. Just as salt brings out the flavor in food, your words, actions, and spirit can bring out the best in those around you. When you live with gratitude, kindness, and faith, you infuse life with a richness that others can taste and experience. Like salt, you'll bring flavor to the people around you in such a way that they too will begin to enjoy life like they've never done before. Don't just go through the motions, let your spirit dance, let your heart overflow with hope, and let your joy be contagious. When you choose to live fully, generously, and with a playful spirit, those around you begin to taste life in a new way. They start to smile more, hope more, and embrace the beauty of today as they never have before.

Jesus gives us all a warning in Matt. 5:13. He said that salt that loses its taste is good for nothing but to be cast out. In other words, your life has little or no value if you're not helping to make the lives of other people better. Be careful how you live your life. Like impurities in salt, sin in a man's life will cause him to lose his impact in the world. Making a lasting impact depends more on how you live your life than on the words you speak. It's true, actions speak louder than words. Be a light that shines brightly. The light of Christ within you shines so that others can see and glorify Him. Light is clear and pure. All a light does is shine. God wants you to be that kind of believer, a light that is pure and shines for His glory. When your light is shining as bright as God wants it to shine, people will feel closer to God when they're with you. They're impacted by your life, your smile, your countenance, your joy, your friendliness, your positive attitude about everything.

God doesn't give us a voice, a platform, or a position so we can be seen, but so others can see Him through us. God delights in a life that spreads His goodness. By being the flavor, He designed you to be, you are not just living, you are awakening others to the abundant life he intended for them. True influence is a sacred trust. It is the light He places in our hands so we can shine it into someone else's darkness. It is the encouragement we speak that lifts a weary soul. It is the wisdom we share that helps someone take their next step toward wholeness. When God increases your influence, He is inviting you to participate in His work - shaping hearts, healing wounds, and inspiring change. Influence becomes powerful when it is surrendered to Him. It becomes meaningful when it serves others. And it becomes eternal when it reflects His love. Use your influence intentionally. Let it strengthen the weak, comfort the hurting, guide the searching, and uplift the discouraged.

The purpose of influence is to make a positive change in people's lives. In God's kingdom, influence is not about how many people follow you; it's about how many lives are better because you followed Him. Having influence is both a responsibility and a privilege. God wants you to exert that power within you to help people grow in their understanding of God and to influence them to live a godly life. When you walk into a room, does the atmosphere change? Is there something about you that makes people take notice? If so, that's influence. Influence is potency, the ability to bring about a particular result. How potent are you? Do you have great strength and influence in a moral sense? The word "potent" means 'having or wielding force, authority, or influence.' It means to be all powerful, to be strong enough to transform the human heart. A person who is potent is very effective and powerful. Don't waste your time doing things where you are not effective, where you don't have an influence.

In every generation, God raises up people who refuse to run from problems - they run toward them. A person's value is not measured by what they avoid, but by what they confront with faith, wisdom, and courage. Problems are not evidence of weakness; they are invitations to rise into the purpose God placed inside you. Your value is seen when you step into the challenges others dismiss. David did not become a king because he played the harp; he became a king because he solved a problem named Goliath. Joseph was not exalted in Egypt for his dreams alone, but because he interpreted Pharaoh's dilemma and offered a divine solution that saved a nation. Daniel was promoted not because he blended in, but because he carried God's wisdom into situations no one else could resolve. God uses difficulty to reveal the strength, creativity, insight, and resilience He planted in you. Every time you solve a problem - big or small - you display the nature of the God who created order out of chaos.

Do not fear the mountain in front of you. Do not curse the obstacles in your path. The very things that intimidate others may be the platforms God will use to elevate you. When you solve the problem, you become the answer someone has been praying for. A follower of God does not seek comfort, they seek purpose. And purpose is always connected to solving problems that bring glory to God and blessing to others. So when life presents you with challenges, lift your head. This is your moment. This is where your value shines. Let God's wisdom guide you, let His strength sustain you, and let His Spirit empower you to do what others cannot. You were born to be a solution to somebody's problem. Remember, influence is measured by the changes that are made to what you're exposed to. An impact is made when you pour your influence into the situation at hand. With influence, people and their circumstances will not be the same as before you arrived on the scene.

Your presence should cause a positive change to happen. That's influence. That's making an impact on the situation at hand. The purpose of your life is to help make this world a better place. A person's value is based on the problems they solve. How you handle a crisis determines how people see you. It's what determines how much of an impact you'll have. What you say in a storm changes how people see you, how they respect you. You gain influence when you remain strong under pressure. You can stay strong in a trial when you have the confidence you're doing what you were created to do. View chaos and adversity as an opportunity for you to make an impact on this world. It's during times of trial when your light should shine the brightest. You are called to thrive in an environment of conflict. Because of who you are in Christ, you can be convinced you can make an impact on the world. If you're not convinced, then the enemy has already defeated you.

Know who you are in Christ. You can't be an external light until you first have internal light. Pray for the eyes of your understanding to be enlightened (Eph. 1:18). This is how you have influence which is the currency of impact and purpose. Can your influence increase? Absolutely! Luke 2:52 says, "And Jesus increased in wisdom and stature, and in favor with God and man." Acts 10:38 says He was always going about helping people and doing good for God was with Him. He touched people's lives wherever He went. His influence was everywhere. The memory of His love and concern for people is still talked about today. You, also, should show genuine interest in others. Smile and let people know you care about them. Treat everyone with kindness and respect. Be proactive as you strive to make an impact on the world. Don't sit back but in love engage in the lives of others. Be there when they need you. Be a friend they can count on.

God told Abraham, "I will bless you and make your name great and you shall be a blessing" (Gen. 12:1,2). In other words, God commanded Abraham to impact the world. He's commanding you to do the same thing. He'll bless you, make your name great, and then He'll send you out to influence the lives of other people. God's blessings are never meant to stop with you - they're meant to flow through you. When God places His hand on your life, He does more than lift you; He prepares you. He strengthens you in the secret place, increases your capacity, and enlarges your vision. God intends to do a work in you that becomes a work through you. As you step forward and do what God has called you to do, He'll bless you and increase your influence. You'll make an impact wherever you go. Hunger and thirst for the chance to make a positive impact on the world. This is important because your hunger is an indication of your future. God is no respecter of persons. If He blessed Abraham, He'll bless you. If He used Abraham to change the world, He'll also use you to change the world.

You are blessed, you are chosen, and you are sent into the world so that someone else can find hope through your life. When God blesses you, He is not merely decorating your life - He is equipping your purpose. When He makes your name great, He is not inflating your ego - He is expanding your influence. And when He sends you out, it is because there are lives waiting on the other side of your obedience. God raises you so you can lift others. He teaches you so you can guide others. He heals you so you can comfort others. He blesses you so you can bless others. Don't hide what God has put in you. Don't shrink back from the doors He opens. When God elevates you, it's a signal that your mission is about to begin. Step forward in faith, knowing that every blessing you carry is a tool in God's hand to change the world around you. You were never meant to stand still. Faith moves. Faith reaches. Faith steps out into the unknown trusting that God has already gone ahead of you.

Step forward in faith not because you have everything figured out, and not because the path is perfectly clear - but because God has already placed something within you that the world needs. Every blessing you carry, every gift, every experience, every lesson learned - none of it is accidental. These are tools in the hands of a Master Builder. When you take that step—however small—it becomes a doorway through which God releases His purpose. So walk boldly. Walk confidently. Walk with expectation. The blessings in your life are not ornaments; they are instruments. They are not just for you to enjoy, but for God to use to shape, lift, heal, and inspire those around you. When you place what you have into His hands, it becomes more than a blessing - it becomes a catalyst for change. Today, step forward in faith. Offer God what's in your hands. And watch Him transform it into something eternal. Go forward and watch the world become a better place because you are in it.

Why were you born? You're not here just to work long hours and pay bills. You're here to change the world. You weren't born to make a living, you were born to make a difference. You're here to change the world from the way you entered it. The key to making a difference in the world is influence which is the capacity and ability to affect and effect circumstances and the environment you are in. A command often forgotten in what Jesus said in Matt. 28:19, "Go into all the world and make disciples of every nation." The Greek word for "world" is "cosmos" and it means 'governing powers' or 'systems of control.' This word refers to the political world, the banking system, the insurance system, the education system, the entertainment system, and the world of sports. Christ said to go into these systems and make disciples of them. The word "disciple" is not a religious word; it's a word from the field of education. The word "disciple" simply means 'student' or 'learner.'

This word implies that you cannot disciple someone unless you are their teacher. That being said, you cannot be a teacher unless you are in a position of influence. You can't teach those whom you cannot influence. You cannot influence students unless you are in a position of power and have knowledge they do not have. Jesus said He wants you to be a teacher and the world around you is to be the students you influence. Sad to say, the church is losing the world very fast. They're too busy trying to get people to feel good that they're not training them to impact the world. Discipleship is all about you becoming a person of influence. People will listen to you because of your expertise, your experience, and your knowledge but that is not the whole story. What truly opens hearts is the anointing of God upon your life. Your skill and what you've been through may gain attention, but it is the Spirit of God within you that brings transformation.

Every lesson you've learned, every trial you've endured, every victory you've walked through has shaped your voice. Your experience has given you authority. Your knowledge has given you clarity. Your expertise has given you confidence. But it is God's presence that gives your words power. When you speak from a place of humility and surrender, people don't just hear you - they feel you. They sense the wisdom forged in the fire. They recognize the authenticity of someone who has walked with God through real battles. So keep growing. Keep learning. Keep deepening your walk with the Lord. Because when expertise meets anointing, when experience meets grace, and when knowledge meets revelation - your voice becomes a tool God uses to lift others, strengthen believers, and draw hearts closer to Him. You are not just speaking from your head; you are speaking from your journey. And that is why people will listen.

When you know what you're talking about, people will listen to you. They'll become your students, and you'll have an impact on their life. Notice that Joseph said God "has made me a father to Pharaoh" (Gen. 45:8). He was a young man but God gave him great influence over the older Pharaoh. Joseph changed all the laws of Egypt, and he influenced Pharaoh to decree that all the people should worship God and God alone. That's called influence, power, expertise, and knowledge. You can't disciple people unless you have influence over them. God took you out of eternity and placed you in a body so you could influence this present generation. He wants you to make an impact. Don't confuse influence with fame and popularity. Marilyn Monroe is still famous today, but she has no influence in the world. Having influence does not mean you will be popular. Jesus was not popular but His impact on the world is alive and well today.

One of the greatest secrets in life is that your worth is based on how you are valued. If you have little value on your job, you won't make much money there. How do you get more pay? You increase your value to the company. You become unique by becoming significant by becoming rare. When you become rare, people will seek you out. They'll come looking for you the same way people dig for diamonds and oil. How do you become rare? By refining the gift God placed inside of you. Continue to work on perfecting your gift until you become like nobody else. To become rare, you must master something. You must be able to do what no one else can do to the degree that you do it. You will refine what you invest in. Take all the time you need to develop and perfect the gift inside you. Do that and you'll become rare and valuable to others. People will not seek you out if all you are is average and mediocre. They're looking for something unique, something rare, qualities that no one else has.

Invest in yourself and you'll soon be an influence on others. God will do for you "exceedingly abundantly above all that you ask or think" (Eph. 3:20). How will He do this? "According to the power that works in you" (vs. 20). The power to impact the world resides in your inner man. Your ability to influence others is activated by God's mighty power working inside you. You'll be able to do more than you can request in prayer or conceive by way of anticipation. Refine your gift and yield to the Spirit inside you. By doing that there will be no limit to what God can do in you and through you. Prov. 18:16 says, "A man's gift makes room for him, and brings him before great men." Your gift will bring you opportunities to influence others. All it takes to influence somebody is one word of encouragement, one genuine expression of love, one caring moment to offer someone a helping hand. Don't waste your influence. "Let your light shine before others that they may see your good deeds and glorify your Father in heaven" (Matt. 5:16).

Life is too short to have your influence wasted. You were created for influence so make it your aim to make a maximum impact on the world. Don't just pass through life but make your mark in the quicksand of time. Life for you should not be how long you live but how well you live. Don't be just a passerby in life. Make your life count. Be a blessing to your generation. Maximize your life and live out your full potential. You'll have influence when you discover why you're here. You were created with purpose, designed by God with gifts, dreams, and abilities that no one else can carry. The discovery of divine purpose helps you to know what to invest your life in and where. Set your face on your purpose and you'll be able to make maximum impact on the world. Set your face on what is needful and not on what is convenient. Maximize your life -

lean into growth, walk in purpose, and let God's power turn your potential into impact.

| 4 |

"A LIFE LIVED WELL"

The original purpose of God is to manifest the influence of heaven's culture on earth through colonizing earth with the kingdom of heaven. From the beginning, God's desire was never simply to place humanity on earth and leave us to find our own way. His original purpose has always been far deeper, far more magnificent. God intended for the culture of heaven with its values, its order, its purity, its peace, its love, and its righteousness to be manifested on earth through His children. Earth was designed to be a reflection of heaven's reality. When God created humanity in His image, He placed within us the capacity to carry His nature, to demonstrate His character, and to extend His kingdom. We were meant to be His ambassadors, His representatives, His extension. In other words, God's plan was to colonize earth with the kingdom of heaven - not through force or domination, but through influence, transformation, and the power of His Spirit working in and through willing hearts.

Heaven's culture is a culture of life. It is a culture where the will of God is the atmosphere, where love is the language, where worship is the lifestyle, and where righteousness is the foundation. When Jesus taught us to pray, "Your kingdom come, Your will be done on earth as it is in heaven," He wasn't giving us poetic words - He was revealing the original mission. He was calling us back to God's first intention. In other words, godly influence is tethered to God's purpose. It takes influence for God's will to be done on earth as it is in heaven. What is influence? It's the capacity to cause other people to listen to you or to follow you. It's the force of impression of one thing on another. A divine truth of vital importance is that every human being ever born was created by God to be an influence on the earth. Sad to say, most people die without influencing anybody, and this includes their home, their church, their neighborhood, and their workplace.

The kingdom of heaven is not merely a destination we hope to reach someday; it is a reality we are called to manifest today. Every act of love, every choice of righteousness, every word of truth, every display of compassion, every moment of obedience is a seed of heaven planted in the soil of earth. Through us, God's influence spreads. Through us, heaven touches earth. And when heaven touches earth, darkness retreats. Bondage breaks. Healing flows. Peace replaces fear. Order overcomes chaos. Because the kingdom isn't just an idea - it's a power, a presence, and a culture that transforms everything it encounters. So walk with purpose. Live with intention. Recognize that God has placed you here not merely to survive but to bring heaven's reality into earthly places. Let your life be a window through which the world can see what heaven looks like. You are a carrier of the Kingdom, chosen to manifest God's original purpose: to reveal the influence of heaven on earth.

In simple terms, the word "influence" means 'to dominate in life.' A person of influence dominates the environment they are in. There is a spiritual force in their life that makes people look up when they enter a room. They respect that person and want to hear what they have to say. Whoever dominates an area of life will have influence on planet earth. Their impact on the world will remain long after they're dead. Influence means you have so much dominion that even death can't destroy it. The impact of what you do should go on and on. We only have one life to live on this earth and we must spend our time here wisely. There is nothing worse than a wasted life. Jesus said to "let your light shine among men" (Matt. 5:16). The most effective way to make maximum impact is a life lived well. 1 Peter 2:12 says, "Keep your behavior excellent among the Gentiles." MSG, "Live an exemplary life among the natives so that your actions will refute their prejudices."

Peter is saying you are to reveal your integrity wherever you go. The world craves to see people who will do what they say they will do. Integrity is not something you put on and take off like clothing. It is the quiet, steady light within you that God intends for the world to see. Wherever you walk, whatever room you enter, and whoever you interact with, your life is meant to reflect the character of Christ. The world is hungering desperately for people whose words mean something, whose actions carry weight, and whose promises stand firm even when it costs them. When you choose integrity, you choose to honor God above convenience, reputation, or personal gain. You choose to let your "yes" mean "yes" and your "no" mean "no." You choose to live in such a way that people don't have to guess who you are or question what you stand for - they can see it clearly, consistently, and confidently. Your integrity is your testimony. It's a sermon you preach without speaking. It's a witness that reaches places your voice may never go.

You'll be able to influence others when they see you shunning evil and abstaining from fleshly lusts that war against the soul (1 Peter 2:11). Do good wherever you go. Live a noble life that is characterized by inward purity and an outward quality. In other words, let your light shine. What does the world see when they gaze upon you? Ruth Graham used to say, "A saint is a person who makes it easy to believe in Jesus." People of God should be the most honorable, honest, faithful, trustworthy, and reliable people in the community. This is how maximum impact is made. Remember why you're here. The ultimate goal and purpose of living a life of integrity is what it will do to the world around you.1 Peter 2:12 says, "They will see your honorable behavior, and they will give honor to God when He judges the world." Think about that. By living a life of integrity, you will influence non-believers to give honor to and glorify God. There is no bigger and better impact than that.

Life is short and it's crucial that you be intentional in how you live. You are called to impact the world and to influence others. You are not placed on this earth to drift aimlessly or to simply survive the passing of days. God designed you with purpose, intention, and divine assignment. Every breath you take is a reminder that heaven has invested something valuable in you, something meant to influence others and bring light into dark places. The motive of living a life of positive impact is to please God and glorify His name (Matt. 6:33). Your highest priority is to please God and profit His kingdom. It is imperative that you live your life in a way that will result in having a maximum impact on those around you. How can you live your life for maximum impact? First, serve the Lord with humility (Acts 20:19). Having a servant's heart takes a mindset of humility. Phil. 2:3 (NLT) says, "Don't be selfish; don't try to impress others. Be humble, thinking of others as better than yourself."

God placed you here on purpose, for a purpose. You are called to impact the world, not blend into it. You are called to influence others, not shrink back from the opportunity to lead by example. Serving the Lord is essentially serving others. Vs. 4 says, "Don't look out only for your own interests, but also for the interest of others." Jesus, also, was humble. Phil. 2:7 says, "He gave up His divine privilege; He took the humble position of a servant and was born a human being." When you serve others, you are demonstrating in a very real and powerful way that life is not just about us. It's about Jesus Christ and it's about others and their needs. Also, grow in your knowledge of Christ so you can share Him with others. Paul said, "I never shrank back from telling you what you needed to hear" (Acts 20:20). You can influence others by showing them by your example what being a Christ follower is all about. Live out what you say you believe.

When you live intentionally - aligning your choices with God's will - you become a vessel through which His love, wisdom, and power are revealed. Because life is brief, it is crucial that you live with intention. Don't wait for "the right season" or "a better time." The right time is now. Someone is watching your faith. Someone is strengthened by your courage. Someone is transformed because you chose to obey God when it would have been easier to stay silent or stay still. So live with clarity. Live with conviction. Live with eternity in mind. Make every day count, because every day carries eternal potential. Every day you can touch a life and every life you touch echoes beyond anything you can see. You matter. Your influence matters. Your purpose matters. Walk boldly in it. You are not here by accident, and neither are the people who cross your path. Heaven writes moments into your day where a word, a smile, a prayer, or a simple act of kindness can touch a life in ways you may never fully know.

You impact the world by living a life of sacrifice, by sacrificing what you want for the benefit of others. You are to bless others despite personal expense. Rom. 12:1 says you are to "present your bodies a living sacrifice, holy, acceptable to God which is your reasonable service." 2 Cor. 5:15 says, "Those who live should live no longer for themselves, but for Him who died for them and rose again." Paul said, "I do not count my life dear to myself" (Acts 20:24). Be like Paul and view your life as a gift to be used to magnify Christ and to influence others. Your calling is to be a source of inspiration and encouragement to others. You're here to influence people to be better than they were before you encountered them. You were created for positive impact, to add value to the lives of others. You're here to promote the well-being of people wherever you go. Your mission is to fill the world with love, joy, peace, and happiness to all those within the range of your influence.

Let your biggest joy be in doing good to others. Find true happiness in blessing those around you for, indeed, it is more blessed to give than to receive. The world waits for the manifestation of your presence. Ask God to use you to be the answer to the problem someone is complaining about. You were created to make a positive difference in this world. Your impact is measured by the vacuum your absence creates. What this means is that when people spend time with you, they'll walk away transformed. We are all commanded to love people as God loves them. We are called to help the hurting and to proclaim forgiveness to the broken and new life to the lost. God calls us to change the world for the good. The positive impact we are to make on others comes from the reality of Christ living in us and through us. To impact the world, you must be a person of diligence. Do whatever it takes to influence other people. Work hard as you proclaim the gospel and minister to their needs.

With steady, earnest, and energetic effort do what needs to be done even if it's not convenient for you. Go out of your way to bless others. People who are diligent get the job done. They're persistent in what they do and don't quit until they have given it their all. Paul urged Timothy to "be diligent in these matters; give yourself wholly to them, so that everyone may see your progress" (1 Tim. 5:15). Be diligent setting an example for others "in speech, in conduct, in love, in faith, and in purity" (vs. 12). All actions flow from the posture of our hearts. When you are diligent in everything you do, you'll set a standard that will impact the world around you. 2 Peter 1:10 (NLT), "Work hard to prove that you really are among those God has called and chosen. Do these things, and you will never fall away." In order to make a difference you need to be willing to work diligently. Your passion for the work of God must be stronger than your desire for worldly things.

You must be willing to make sacrifices, to do what is not convenient. You need to rearrange your preferences and do everything for the kingdom of God. Also, you must be consistent in the things you do. Consistency flows from having a deep commitment to God. You devote yourself wholly to Him (Matt. 6:24) and seek His kingdom above everything else (vs. 33). Be like the Lord who said in Mal. 3:6, "For I am the Lord, I change not." Consistency is the key to any relationship of trust. John Maxwell said, "Solid trust can develop only when people can trust you all the time." God's nature is characterized by consistency. James 1:17 (NLT) says, "He never changes or casts a shifting shadow." Heb. 13:8 says Jesus is "the same yesterday, today, and forever." God is consistent, reliable, and dependable in all things and He calls all men to demonstrate consistency in their faith, service, and witness (1 Peter 1:15). Paul urges all believers to "live a life worthy of the calling you have received (Eph. 4:1).

Life is hard and people need someone to stand by their side during difficult times. They need people to encourage them, comfort them, and urge them on. The storms of life come without warning, things like disappointment, loss, betrayal, pressure, and pain. And while we trust God to carry us through, He often uses people as instruments of His comfort and support. That's why people who are hurting need someone who will stand by their side - not those who are perfect, but those who are faithful. Be a person who shows up when life gets messy, a person who prays with people when they don't even have the strength to pray for themselves. Those who are overcome by the struggles of life need someone who will speak life into them when everything around them feels empty. They need people who hold up their arms like Aaron and Hur held up the arms of Moses when the battle grew fierce. A godly man's presence reminds people that they are not walking through the valley alone.

Life can feel overwhelming, and everyone needs someone who will stay close through the struggles - someone to speak hope, offer comfort, and help them keep moving forward. Use your courage to strengthens theirs. Allow your faith to become a shield when theirs are too heavy to carry. Trust God to use the wisdom He gives you to bring clarity to those who are hurting, when confusion surrounds them on all sides. Use your love to reflect the heart of God - a love that stays, protects, and believes. Life is overwhelming for some people right now so don't let them suffer alone. Be there for them during their time of need. Pray for God to send you to those who are hurting. Go out of your way and stand by their side. Walk with them, pray with them, believe with them, and listen to them. Sometimes a listening ear is the greatest gift you can give a person who is hurting. In a world full of struggle, one of the deepest blessings a person can receive is a friend who refuses to let them fight alone.

Helping others live a better life is rarely easy. True ministry - real, Christ-centered service - costs us something. It stretches us, inconveniences us, and often pushes us far beyond what feels comfortable. When we step into someone else's darkness, we carry a bit of the weight they've been struggling under. When we lift a brother or sister who has fallen, we feel the strain in our own souls. And when we choose to love those who are difficult to love, we expose our own hearts to misunderstanding, rejection, and weariness. But this is exactly why Scripture calls us to "endure hardship as a good soldier of Jesus Christ" (2 Timothy 2:3). We are not serving for applause, comfort, or recognition - we serve for Christ. We endure for His sake. We press on because His love compels us, His Spirit strengthens us, and His example leads us. Jesus did not call us to an easy path; He called us to a meaningful one. He endured the cross not because it was simple, but because it was necessary. And when we carry the burdens of others, we are walking in His footsteps - loving the way He loved, giving the way He gave, and persevering the way He persevered.

When helping becomes exhausting, when your kindness is taken for granted, and when the weight feels heavier than you expected, always remember that every sacrifice offered in the name of Jesus carries eternal value. Every hardship endured to lift another soul is seen by the Father. And every moment of perseverance brings you closer to the heart of Christ Himself. Don't walk away but keep going, keep loving, and keep serving. Why? Because someone's breakthrough may be on the other side of your endurance. And Christ, who endured everything for you, will strengthen you to endure everything for Him. Your faithfulness in the storm is not just about what God is doing for you, it's also about what He's doing through you. When you keep standing, keep believing, and keep pressing forward despite the pressure, you become a living testimony of God's sustaining power. Your endurance becomes their inspiration. Your persistence becomes their proof that God really does care for His people. Your resilience becomes the spark that ignites their own hope.

There is a cry from the heart of every true believer for a life that is higher than money or popularity or worldly success. Inside the heart of every child of God is a cry for the miraculous, for signs and wonders, for the opportunity to make a maximum impact on the world. The word "maximum" means 'greatest in quantity or highest in degree attainable; the most; the best.' The word "impact" means 'affect; influence.' Push yourself to live your life to the highest degree attainable and this will allow you to influence others with the force of a maximum life. Life is too short to be wasted. Life is not measured in its duration but in its donation. Making a maximum impact is the best goal to pursue while alive. Fulfill your God-given destiny by making maximum impact in life according to the will of God by being a blessing to the world around you. It is your calling and responsibility to love God wholeheartedly, love others sacrificially, and make disciples for His kingdom. This is how you impact the world.

| 5 |

"CITY ON A HILL"

God didn't form you by accident or place you on this earth without purpose. Heaven designed you with intention, with gifts, with influence, and with a voice that carries weight in the lives of others. You were created to make a difference - not just to exist, but to leave a mark that reflects the goodness and love of God. Because of that, keep your heart impact-minded. Wake up each day knowing that someone's life can be changed by your encouragement, your kindness, your obedience, your boldness, or simply your presence. Don't shrink back. Don't hide your light. Don't underestimate what God can do through a willing vessel. The world may seem loud and chaotic, but that's exactly why your impact is needed. Be willing to engage in the world around you. Don't be like a hermit who lives in a cave somewhere. Go out into the world where problems run rampant knowing that you can do all things through Christ who strengthens you (Phil. 4:13).

Impact doesn't happen in isolation. It happens when you step out, when you listen, when you serve, when you love, when you speak truth, and when you carry the presence of God into everyday places. Let your life be a living expression of Christ's compassion and power. You were made to shine. You were made to influence. You were made for impact. So go forward today with intention. Live on purpose and let the world feel the weight of the God who works through you. God will give you the strength to impact this world and influence others. You'll be able to do anything and everything God asks you to do. People who live their lives for maximum impact wake up each morning and say, "Lord, let me help somebody today and be a blessing to them." Paul said he served God and others "so that I may finish my race with joy" (Acts 20:24). Living your life as a living sacrifice brings incredible meaning and joy to your life so live your life for the purpose of being a blessing to somebody else.

When you live a life of sacrifice, your life has maximum impact. There is no greater joy then this. John Maxwell said, "To make a positive impact on your world, you need to become a person of influence. Without influence, there is no success." What is influence? it's the capacity to have an effect on the character, development, or behavior of someone or something. You have the God-given capacity to alter the state of people, places, and things. With godly influence you can impact the world. With influence you can be fruitful and multiply (Gen. 1:28). This means you can determine, decide, control, guide, shape, or govern the environment you are in. God has literally made you an agent of change. The world around you will never be the same because you are in it. Jesus said you are the salt of the earth (Matt. 5:13) and this means you bring flavor to the world around you. Life just seems better when you're around. Suddenly things don't seem as bad as they were before you arrived on the scene.

The Message Bible says "Let me tell you why you are here. You're here to be salt-seasoning that brings out the God-flavors of this earth. If you lose your saltiness, how will people taste godliness? You've lost your usefulness and will end up in the garbage." The flavor that God has put in you is what will impact the lives of those around you. Let people everywhere taste the goodness that is inside of you. People will value you to the degree that you can add value to them. This isn't a call to perform for approval, nor is it a measure of your worth in God's eyes. Your worth is already settled in heaven. But it is a reminder that the influence God gives you on earth is connected to the seeds you sow in the lives of others. A poor man is not a person with no money; he's a person who is not adding value to others. Greatness is not achieved through position, but through contribution. Your impact grows in the same measure that your willingness to serve grows. Keep adding value where you can. Speak life, offer wisdom, share hope, serve with humility, love intentionally.

The more you invest in others, the more God invests in you. And the more you pour out, the more He pours into your life. Remember: your value is not determined by people, but your influence in their lives is shaped by how you bless them. Your value on this planet is based on your flavor, on your saltiness. You hold the promise of positive change for others. If you don't fulfill that promise, if you lose your flavor, you'll "be thrown out and trampled underfoot by men" (Matt. 5:13). Never lose sight that you have inside of you the capacity to affect the lives of other people. Why? Because on this earth you are an extension of God. There is a piece of God inside of you which you are to pour into the lives of other people. Invite them to "taste and see that the Lord is good" (Ps. 34:8). This simple invitation is more than poetry - it's a call for people to experience God for themselves. It invites them to taste, to personally sample the goodness, mercy, and faithfulness of the Lord.

Let the presence of God radiate out of you like never before. Be ecstatic as you go around expressing overwhelming happiness and joyful excitement. Happiness is an emotion arising from an inner conviction that all is right in your walk with God. It's a sense of well-being, joy, and contentment. The flavor of God inside of you is what you use to influence people, places, and things. Live in such a way that people will discover and celebrate your flavor. Recognize and celebrate your flavor. Whether you realize it or not, there is somebody out there who needs your influence in their life. Your mission as a person of influence is not to get others to think more highly of you. Your mission is to get people to think more highly of themselves. All around you people are hungry for encouragement, recognition, security, and hope. Give these people what they need so they can reach their full potential. People are hungry for love and it's your responsibility to give it to them.

Your impact on people is directly related to the depth of your love and concern for them. Everyone needs to feel valued. Tell people how important they are. Give them a pat on the back and tell them how much they mean to you. Encourage people by telling them they're better than they think they are. The ability to influence is a by-product of encouragement. Be a giver and add value to people's lives. Give them love, honor, and respect. Create an environment where they can flourish in today's world. This is how maximum impact is made. You'll be able to influence people when you appreciate them for who they are and what they are. Columnist George M. Adams called encouragement "oxygen to the soul." People come alive when you encourage them. It makes them listen to what you have to say. Just as salt does no good unless it comes in contact with food, so must you be in contact with and be accessible to those you wish to influence.

Love always finds a way to help but you must do it up close. You can't nurture and influence people from a distance. Get personal with people. Enhance their lives by reaching out to them. Lift them up and inspire them. Motivate them to become all they were created to be. The truth is that most people don't have faith in themselves. A lack of self-esteem holds them back more than the trials they encounter. Encourage people and deliberately help them to succeed. Have faith in them and your influence will soon have them having faith in themselves. Faith has a way of multiplying. When you choose to believe in someone - even when they can't yet see their own potential - you become a living reminder of God's grace at work. Your confidence in them becomes a seed planted in their heart. And seeds, when nurtured through love, patience, and prayer, always grow. So keep encouraging. Keep uplifting.

Keep speaking life. Your influence may be the very thing God uses to awaken courage, hope, and identity in another soul.

Believe in people and soon they will believe in who God created them to be. Become a life coach to others. Walk beside them and give them the guidance they need. Teach them the ins and outs of life. John Maxwell said, "Become a believer in people, and even the most tentative and inexperienced people can bloom right before your eyes." When you believe in people, they'll do the impossible. They'll rise to meet your level of expectations for them. They'll go the extra mile to do their best. Marshal John H. Spalding said, "Those who believe in our ability do more than stimulate us. They create for us an atmosphere in which it becomes easier to succeed." Encourage people to dream big dreams. Help them to expand their horizons and motivate them to move to a whole new level of living. You will never find the definition of success for your own life until you first help those people God sends to you find success in their own life.

Author Alan Loy McGinnes said, "There is no more noble occupation in the world than to assist another human being, to help someone succeed." Helping others succeed is one of the most incredible things you can ever do. Jesus gave up who He was so His followers could become who they could never be on their own. John 12:24 says, "Unless a grain of wheat falls into the ground and dies, it remains alone, but if it dies, it produces much grain." There are seasons in life when God invites us to a deeper kind of surrender - one that goes beyond comfort, beyond preference, and even beyond the quiet desires we hold inside. It is the surrender that allows our wants and wishes to be crushed for the sake of others. The olive is crushed to get oil, and the grape is crushed to get wine. Allow your wants and desires to be crushed for the sake of others. Your sacrifice for others will help them grow exceedingly. Columnist Denis Waitley said, "The greatest achievements are those that benefit others."

When you influence people to raise their level of living, you'll brighten their future and increase their potential for success. When you choose to lay down what you want so that someone else can rise - when you set aside your own desires so that another can find peace, healing, or hope - you are walking in the very footsteps of Jesus, who surrendered His will out of love for a world that did not yet understand Him. In these moments of dying to self, something sacred happens. Your heart grows softer, your spirit grows stronger, and your character becomes more like Christ. Self-sacrifice is not about losing yourself. It is about letting God shape you into someone who loves beyond themselves. Someone who sees the needs of others as holy ground. So when the Lord asks you to yield, to give up, to let go -trust Him and do it. Your surrender becomes someone else's blessing. Your sacrifice becomes someone else's breakthrough. And in the end, what you give up for love, God returns in ways far greater than you could ever imagine.

Jesus used the concepts of salt and light a number of different times to refer to the role of His followers in the world. He said in Matt. 5:13, "You are the salt of the earth." Salt had two purposes in the Middle East of the first century. Because of the lack of refrigeration, salt was used to preserve food, especially meat which could quickly spoil in the desert environment. People of God are called to be preservatives to the world, preserving it from ungodly people whose unredeemed natures are corrupted by sin. Second, salt was used then, and now, as a flavor enhancer. In like manner, we are all called to enhance the flavor of life in this world. All men are called to influence the world for good the same way salt has a positive influence on the flavor of the food it seasons. Where there is strife, we are to be peacemakers. When people are sorrowful, we are to bind up their wounds. Where there is hatred, we are to exemplify the love of God in Christ.

Jesus then said, "You are the light of the world. A city that is set on a hill cannot be broken" (Matt. 5:14). Jesus is saying that the good works of the people of God are to shine for all to see. Why? Because the presence of light in darkness is something that is unmistakable. Your good works must be evident for all to see. Vs. 16, "Let your light so shine before men, that they may see your good works and glorify your Father in heaven." Notice carefully that salt and light never exist for themselves. Salt does not boast of its flavor, and light does not shine to draw attention to its own glow. Salt exists to enhance, to preserve, to heal. Light exists to reveal, to guide, to warm, and to push back the darkness. In the same way, God did not call you to live for yourself, He called you to be salt that brings out the goodness around you, and light that helps others see their way. Your purpose is fulfilled when someone's burden becomes lighter, when someone's path becomes clearer, when someone's heart becomes encouraged.

Salt works quietly. Light works naturally. Neither demands applause. They simply do what they were created to do - make things better. So today, choose to be a blessing without needing recognition. Let your kindness season someone's life. Let your compassion shine into someone's darkness. Because when your life lifts others, you are fulfilling the very reason Jesus called you the salt of the earth and the light of the world. Be like salt and help preserve and enhance the lives of other people. Be like light which is a means of illumination. Be a light by which people see the things of God. Light makes other things visible. It brings beautiful things to light. Influence people by letting them see how wonderful a walk with God is. Be like a city set on a hill. Long before maps were drawn up people would use a city on a hill for navigation purposes. They would plan their route for a journey based on a certain landmark such as a mountain or a city set on a hill.

Likewise, God wants to use you to give proper direction to the lives of others. Without a city on a hill, the people wouldn't know where they were going. Travelers would lose their sense of direction, causing them to wander without guidance, without clarity, without hope. In the same way, God desires to set you in a visible place - not to elevate your ego, but to illuminate someone else's path. Your life, your testimony, your obedience, and your wisdom are all meant to serve as landmarks to those who are searching. The Lord wants to use your words to steady the confused, your example to inspire the weary, and your faith to anchor the unsure. You may not feel qualified. You may not think your light is bright enough. But God doesn't ask you to be perfect, He asks you to be available.

A lighthouse doesn't try to outshine the sun; it simply shines where it has been placed. And because it shines, ships avoid danger and find safe harbor.

God wants to send you out into the world so you can be a beacon of light for others to follow, a light that illuminates the path people should be on. People are designed by God to be influenced. Prov. 13:20 says, "He who walks with the wise will become wise, but the companion of fools will suffer." People become like the people they hang around with. Draw close to others so you can make a positive difference in their lives. People need to be influenced. When you give them trust by being there when they need you, you'll be able to say, "Imitate me as I imitate Christ" (1 Cor. 11:1). So stand tall. Be willing to be seen. Let God lift your life like a city on a hill. Someone's direction, someone's breakthrough, someone's return to God may depend on the clarity your light provides. Shine with purpose. Shine with humility. Shine because God has positioned you to guide others home.

There should be a passion inside of you to make this world a better place. God changed your life so you can go into the world and help other people's lives be changed. Why are you here? You're here to be salt and light, a city set on a hill. God is not a secret to be kept. By opening up to others, you'll prompt them to open up to God. Matt. 5:15 (MSG), "You don't think I'm going to hide you under a bucket, do you? I'm putting you on a light stand. Now that I've put you on a hilltop, on a light stand - shine! Keep open house; be generous with your lives." The problem in the world today is people have grown accustomed to the darkness. They've grown desensitized to how dark things are. Things that used to make us blush and hide our face in shame are so common to us now that we think nothing about it. A light needs to shine in this darkness of doom and that light is you. Jesus said you are, right now, present tense, the light of the world.

The Greek word for "light" is "phos" and it's where we get the word "photo" from. Jesus is saying you are the photograph of Him in this dark world. You are to be a reflection of the light of the Son of God. His light shines on you and in you so that you can shine forth His light to a spiritually dead world. Your calling is to be a clear picture of who Jesus is to those whose eyes have been darkened by the ravages of sin. Let your light shine. People who commit gross sin are coming out of the closet while Christians are being put in the closet. This is not right. Jesus said don't put your light under a basket but on a lampstand so it gives light to all those who are in the house (Matt. 5:15). Martyn Lloyd-Jones said, "If we find in ourselves a tendency to put the light under a bushel, we must begin to examine ourselves and make sure that it really is light." Letting your light shine means 'to radiate brilliancy.' You're called to shine, to be a beaming light. You're called to provide illumination to those you encounter.

You are like a city on a hill - impossible to hide, impossible to ignore. God has placed His light within you, not to be covered, not to be dimmed, but to shine boldly in the very places where darkness once ruled. You are a living epistle, written not with ink but with the Spirit of the living God. Your life is a message read daily by those around you. You are a living epistle, a walking testimony of the new life that lives in you and shines forth in the darkness. Wherever you go you are illuminating the truth of the gospel by your life because your light is so dramatically different from the darkness of this world. When people see the light of your conduct and character, they'll be drawn to you wanting to know what makes you so different from everyone else. This is when you'll be able to make a positive impact on their life. You'll be able to influence them to follow the light of Jesus just like you're doing.

You may not always realize it, but your words, your actions, your kindness, your endurance, and your faithfulness are preaching louder than any sermon ever spoken from a pulpit. You are a walking testimony of the new life that Christ has birthed within you. The old has passed away; the new has come and that newness radiates with a brilliance no hardship can extinguish. In a world searching for hope, your light is a beacon. In times of confusion, your peace is a compass. In seasons of chaos, your steadfastness reveals the God who never changes. So stand tall. Shine brightly. Let your life speak for you carry the flame of heaven and the darkness cannot overcome it. To impact the world all you have to do is shine forth from whatever lampstand God has strategically placed you on. Your assignment is simple: Let the light of His love, wisdom, and truth radiate from you. Go out into the world and shine, baby, shine!

| 6 |

"COMMON GROUND"

In Matt. 5:13-16, Jesus did not tell you to become salt and light, He said you are already salt and light. You make things better. You make things brighter. You inspire others by doing good things for them in such a way that it calls out of their innermost being the desire to change and get better. Become like Jesus who connected with people wherever He went. He had a remarkable way of meeting people right where they were. He didn't wait for them to clean up their lives or meet a certain standard but instead valued everyone, from the tax collector to the Samaritan woman at the well. He reached out and drew close to the very people society rejected. He touched a leper and showed mercy to the woman caught in adultery. His heart was attentive, His words compassionate, and His presence life changing. When you follow Jesus' example, your life becomes a bridge of compassion. Your words can heal, your presence can comfort, and your actions can demonstrate God's love.

To become like Jesus, you must see people as God sees them. Every person carries a story, a struggle, and a soul in need of grace. When you look beyond labels, you'll see the child of God in everyone. Meet people where they are. Jesus didn't isolate Himself with only the righteous or the learned. He engaged with those society overlooked, judging none, and loving all. Listen and respond with empathy. The power of connection is often found in simple listening. Jesus asked questions, heard hearts, and responded with understanding. Value every encounter. No conversation was too small, no person too insignificant. Each moment was an opportunity to reflect God's love. When you choose to see, value, and love others as Jesus did, you'll become His hands, His voice, and His light in a world that desperately needs Him. When you value them for who they are, and love them as Jesus did, something powerful happens. You become more than a bystander in a hurting world; you become His hands to help, His voice to speak hope, and His light to shine in the darkness.

Every act of kindness, every word of encouragement, every moment of sacrificial love is a reflection of Him. The world doesn't just need advice or opinions; it needs the presence of Christ through you. Let your heart be His heart, your actions His actions, and your life a living testament to His love. Jesus said in Matt. 25:35,36 (MSG), "I was hungry and you fed Me, I was thirsty and you gave Me a drink, I was homeless and you gave Me a room. I was shivering and you gave Me clothes, I was sick and you stopped to visit, I was in prison, and you came to Me." He was then asked, "Master, what are You talking about? When did we ever see you hungry and feed You, thirsty and give You a drink? And when did we ever see You sick or in prison and come to You?" (vs. 37) They're saying, "What are You talking about? We don't understand." Jesus responded, "I'm telling you the truth. Whenever you did one of these things to someone overlooked or ignored, that was Me, you did it to Me" (vs. 40).

When people know you genuinely value them, they'll be open to your influence. They'll cling to you like a magnet and listen to every word you have to say. Your light will shine in the dark areas of their life and they'll be illuminated. They'll see things they were once blinded to. Pray and ask God to show you things of value in another person's life. Listen to Him carefully because you'll see what you are prepared to see. Also, be genuine when you share with people how valuable they are. Be truthful, be real. A phony can be spotted a mile away. It is very important that you back up your words with action. Go to them and ask if there is something you can do to help make their lives better, easier, lighter, or brighter. Listen with an open heart and let your hands and time reflect the compassion your words express. In doing so, you become more than a voice - you become a living example of love in action.

Paul said in 1 Cor. 9:19,22,23 (MSG), "For though I am free from all men, I have made myself a servant to all, that I might win the more. I entered their world and tried to experience things from their point of view. I've become just about every sort of servant there is. I didn't just want to talk about it; I wanted to be in on it." Personal involvement is one of the greatest ways to add value to people. In a world filled with busy schedules and fleeting connections, personal involvement remains one of the most profound ways to add value to someone's life. When you take the time to truly engage with people by listening, encouraging, mentoring, or simply being present with them, you communicate worth and dignity in ways words alone cannot. Acts of involvement, even small ones, are tangible expressions of compassion, love, and service. By investing your time, energy, and heart into others, you become an instrument of God's grace, helping others realize their potential and feel genuinely loved.

Never underestimate the impact of showing up. Your personal touch - whether a word of encouragement, a helping hand, or a listening ear - can transform a life, inspire hope, and create ripples that extend far beyond what you can see. To be personally involved is to add eternal value. You were created in God's image which means the desire to make a positive difference in the world is naturally within you. The desire to impact the world was placed inside of you the day you were created. It was there then and it's still there today. Take all your hopes and dreams and use them to influence others to live a better life, a life beyond what they could ever hope or imagine. Your spirit soars and your morale and enthusiasm climb to new heights when God uses you to make the lives of other people better. Life just feels better when God's will and purpose is fulfilled in your life. Life is great when you feel better about yourself and those around you.

There are people everywhere who need your influence in their life. Know with certainty that the greatest opportunities to impact their lives are ever before you. Never will you run out of people to bless and influence. Submit to God's plan for your life and you'll soon be doing things that make a differ-ence. Your passion to bless people will ignite your spiritual gift and works of service soon follow. This is how you impact the world around you. The time to make a difference is now. Make today count. Don't waste your time and life doing things that have no eternal significance. The secret of your success is determined by what you do daily. Your success is not an acci-dent; it is the result of what you do consistently, day by day. Every small choice, every act of faith, every step of obedience matters. Today is not just another day - it is a gift, a canvas on which God wants you to paint your life with purpose. Today matters because today is all you have.

Paul had a deep passion to impact the world he lived in. If you want to make a similar impact, you must have the same pas-sion he had. Passion is a fire God places within your heart - a longing to serve, to give, and to make a difference in the lives of others. When your passion is rooted in Him, it doesn't lead to selfish ambition or pride; it leads you to become a ser-vant to all. The more you embrace the fire He's given you, the more it fuels humility, patience, and love. True passion trans-forms energy into action, and action into service. Paul's pas-sion changed him. So deep was his passion he said in 1 Cor. 9:20, "To the Jew I became as a Jew, that I might win the Jews." He then said in vs. 22, "To the weak I became as weak, that I might win the weak. I have become all things to all men, that I might by all means save some." Paul was free in Christ, but his passion drove him to become a servant to all. Even Jesus said, "For even the Son of Man did not come to be served, but to serve" (Matt. 20:28).

Passion is not meant to elevate yourself, but to lift others. Let it guide your hands, your words, and your heart toward acts of kindness, encouragement, and selfless love. When passion meets purpose in service, it becomes a reflection of God's own heart for humanity - a light that inspires, heals, and blesses. Paul's passion challenged him to get out of his comfort zone and enter into the world of those he wished to influence. His ministry was not based on how much he knew but on where the people were. You must find them before you can lead them. In other words, you must catch the fish before you clean the fish. And to catch the fish, you must go where the fish are. Paul knew who he was but now he needed to know who the people were. He said, "I entered their world and tried to experience things from their point of view" (1 Cor. 9:22). When you enter their world, you stop trying to force them to agree with your point of view. Instead, you make a diligent effort to learn their point of view.

People often resist connection or understanding until they sense acceptance. Stop trying to move people around. Don't force them to change their lifestyle. Find out where they are and stay with them until they're comfortable. Why is this important? Because people won't be comfortable with you until they know you're comfortable with where they are. Always remember that God calls us to love without pretense, to meet others where they are and not where we wish they were. By entering their world, you send a signal that you're not better than they are. Nothing turns people off more than that. Maintain your integrity and Christlike character around these people and you'll be a light shining in the darkness. These people are now comfortable with you and now you can take them by the hand and slowly lead them to the path they should be on. Be the vessel of grace that reflects God's comfort; your acceptance can become the bridge that leads others closer to Him.

There is always a way to impact the world. All you have to do is "become all things to all men" (1 Cor. 9:22). The key is not in grand gestures or fame, but in the willingness to connect, understand, and serve. Find out where people are at and connect with them there. Be willing to identify with those who don't have the power of understanding to grasp the meaning of the gospel like you do. Becoming all things to all men describes a readiness to accommodate to the customs and habits of the people in order to win a hearing ear for the good news of the gospel. Be willing to stoop to the level of their weakness of comprehension. To save a drowning person sometimes you have to dive into the raging water to reach them. Take the plunge and have the boldness to cross some of the barriers that exist to reach others for Christ. Be like Paul who said, "Woe is me if I don't preach the gospel" (1 Cor. 9:16).

When you step into the lives of others with empathy, humility, and love, you open doors that no force can close. To impact the world, you have to go where the people are so you'll get opportunities to influence them to walk the straight and narrow path. Don't withdraw from these people. Jesus was known as the friend of sinners, but He never compromised His holiness. You are called to do the same. Without a doubt, you need to be distinct in your lifestyle and behavior so that you don't compromise the message you have to give them. Never sacrifice godly principles in your attempt to impact the world. Stay strong in the faith while using every permissible method to help people see the light. John Wesley said, "You need to fear nothing but sin and desire nothing but God. Do that and you will shake the gates of hell and set up the kingdom of heaven on earth." There is always a path - sometimes quiet, sometimes unseen - but it is always there for those willing to walk it in love.

Paul, in his effort to reach people, went anywhere and everywhere, no matter what the situation and surroundings were. He increased his labors and crossed over boundaries of prejudice in race and religion to influence and win men and women for Christ. Be flexible and adaptable as you present your message to others. Jesus talked one way with Nicodemus the Jew and another way to the Samaritan woman at the well. It takes tact to reach people successfully. Tact is the ability to speak the truth in love, knowing when to speak and how to act. It is not compromise; it is wisdom. It is the Holy Spirit guiding your words, your tone, and your actions so that they minister life rather than cause offense. You must be led by the Spirit to know what to say or do to avoid giving offense. The Bible reminds us that words can build up or tear down (Prov. 15:1; Eph. 4:29). To touch hearts without pushing them away, you must be sensitive, discerning, and Spirit-led.

When you are led by the Spirit, you gain insight into hearts and minds. You learn to ask questions rather than dictate, to listen more than lecture, and to respond with gentleness rather than harshness. In doing so, doors that might have been closed by pride or misunderstanding can open, allowing the gospel and godly counsel to take root. Remember, the goal is not to impress, argue, or win debates - it is to reach souls. Tact is the virtue of a person who is understanding and flexible. It enables you to communicate with others in a sensitive and respectful way. As you seek to influence others, pray for discernment, patience, and humility. Let the Spirit guide every word and every gesture, and you will find that even difficult hearts can be touched and lives can be changed. You must have people skills when trying to influence them. Be sensitive when dealing with others. Be diplomatic, thoughtful, considerate, and discrete. Make eye contact and don't cross your arms, don't point, and practice good posture.

Those who are tactful are always careful not to say something hurtful or offensive. They speak calmly and politely and always think before they speak. Tact is the ability to say the right thing at the right time. Sensitive situations are inevitable and how you handle them can make a big difference in the outcome. Take time to think through what you want to say. Be careful not to offend or upset people. Be polite and use words to lift people up and not tear them down. Everybody is different and their circumstances may not be the same. This is why it is required of you to change the elements of your approach when needed. Do what you can to find common ground with people. Listen to them and don't jump into a conversation before hearing what the other person is trying to say. All people appreciate being listened to. When you extend that courtesy to someone, they'll more likely be open to listen to what you have to say.

James 1:19 says, "Be quick to hear, slow to speak, slow to anger." Kindness and respect never go out of style and are appropriate regardless of the subject matter. By listening to people and being kind to them you'll be able to discern where they are spiritually, and this will help you know what to say. To become all things to all people you must be willing to humble yourself, meet people where they're at, and say whatever God tells you to say. Making the adjustment to identify with those you're talking to will cause them to be more open to receive what you have to say. The bottom line is you must connect with people before you can impact their world and bring them into the kingdom. It takes wisdom and creativity to connect with people of various cultures and backgrounds. This is why Prov. 11:30 says, "And he who wins souls is wise." How do you get wise? By hanging around people who don't know Christ and answering all the difficult questions they may ask you.

To catch a fish, you must first bait the hook. You must give the fish something it wants. The same principle applies in your effort to influence people. True influence is not about force or manipulation - it's about understanding what others need, what moves their hearts, and what draws them closer to truth. The truth is, when the world knows you have something they need, they'll hang around you to figure out what it is. Influence rooted in understanding and genuine care has power. Your words, actions, and example become the "bait" that invites others to grow, change, or follow a path of faith. The world is hungry for the knowledge of how to live a better life. Your mission is to understand them enough so you can make them more hungry. Go into their world and say things to stimulate their desire to come into your world. Show them you have the very thing they're looking for. Love these people and live out the gospel message in their presence. Let them see the full benefits of what a relationship with Jesus is really like.

When you seek to guide, teach, or inspire, start by giving something meaningful. Show kindness, wisdom, patience, or encouragement. Offer what resonates with their spirit, not just your own agenda. Just as a fish bites only what appeals to it, people respond to what speaks to their hearts. Remember, God works through those who meet others where they are, offering what is needed, and letting His Spirit do the rest. It's time to stop having Bible studies about how to win people for Christ. In the church people are educated way beyond their level of obedience. The end of the age is fast approaching and it's time to go out into the world and do the things we've been taught in all those studies. The time for action is now! Transformation doesn't come from intellectual teaching but from application. James 1:22 says, "Be doers of the word and not hearers only." You know you're supposed to become all things to all men so go out and become all things to all men. This is how you impact the world around you.

| 7 |

"A BETTER PLACE"

To make an impact in the world you'll need to be more sensitive to the needs of others, to the needs of those in a dark and hurting world. With love and compassion, you need to be willing to step into their pain and suffering and confusion with a posture of empathy, sensitivity, and understanding. Step into the places where people hurt the most. Not with judgment, not with answers already prepared, but with a heart willing to feel what they feel. True ministry, true friendship, true Christlike love is not afraid of someone's pain, someone's suffering, or someone's confusion. Instead, it draws near. It is so important that you be not tone deaf to the world around you. You must be considerate and share the pain and emotions of those who are hurting. You need to weep with those who weep (Rom. 12:15) and be tender-hearted as you share their pain and sorrow with grace and mercy. William Barclay said, "There are few bonds like that of a common sorrow. The bond of tears is the strongest of all."

Sometimes the greatest gift you can give someone is your willingness to sit with them in the darkness until the light returns. To hold their hand when the world feels overwhelming. To remind them, by your presence, that God has not forgotten them. A heartfelt tear can show your love more than a thousand words. It says, "My heart goes out to you. I want to share your pain." Like Jesus you've been sent "to heal the brokenhearted, to preach deliverance to the captives, to set at liberty those who are oppressed" (Luke 4:18). This is a wonderful calling, but it will never be fulfilled until you first become willing to enter the world of the hurting, the world of those in grief and despair. The mercies of God call us to sympathize with others. Listen to what people are saying and take the time to understand what they're going through. If your schedule is interrupted by someone who is hurting, don't look at them as an interruption to your ministry, look at them as the object of your ministry.

Yes, you can make a difference in this world but first you have to increase the level of your sensitivity to the needs of others. Compassion that refuses to get close will never transform a life. Be a person who steps into the storm - not because you have all the answers, but because you carry the heart of the One who does. May your love be courageous, your compassion deep, and your understanding rooted in the grace you yourself have received. Strive to be more like Jesus who was the most sensitive person that's ever lived. Over and over, we read where He looked at people and was moved with compassion for them. He always noticed people and then He'd engage in their world to help them. Because of His sensitivity their lives were never the same. Like Jesus you need to be aware of what's going on around you. If someone looks like they're hurting, go to them and offer to listen to them and help them if you can.

In the midst of hurt and pain you're the hands and feet of Jesus. You're here to be the servant of all so you can be part of helping people during their time of need. Inside of you is the gift of mercy which is the special God-given ability to recognize, empathize, and answer the immediate needs of others. There are hurting people in the world who are counting on you to be merciful to them, to be like the good Samaritan who helped the man beaten and robbed by thieves. You are salt and light and God wants to use you to bind up their wounds, to inspire them with comfort and confidence, to give them hope and a sense of well-being. David said in Ps. 34:18, "The Lord is close to the brokenhearted and saves those who are crushed in spirit." To impact the world, you must do the same thing. It is good to be sensitive to the needs of the world. Weep with those who weep but then rise up and allow your sorrow to propel you to action.

It is amazing how God uses ordinary people to make an extraordinary difference in the lives of the people they come in contact with. Many years ago, a simple, ordinary shoe salesman named Edward Kimball shared the gospel message with a young man who recently came to work at his store. That young man's name was Dwight and in the back room of that store he gave his life to Christ. He later became known as D. L. Moody, one of the greatest evangelists of all time. One day D. L. Moody was preaching and in attendance was a pastor named F. B. Meyer. So stirred was this pastor that he started a nationwide preaching ministry. Later, while Meyer was preaching, a young man named John Wilbur Chapman accepted Christ and later became a well-known traveling evangelist. The work became overwhelming, so he asked a baseball player named Billy Sunday to help him. Billy Sunday later became one of the greatest preachers in the 1900's.

One day Billy Sunday had a revival in North Carolina. When he finished the local people asked an unknown preacher named Mordecai Ham to keep the revival going. Around this time a tall, lanky 16-year-old farmhand came to the meeting and gave his life to Christ. That teenager's name was Billy Graham. Millions of people have been reached by all these preachers, but none of it would have happened without the desire of an ordinary show salesman to make a positive difference in the world. Believe the same thing can happen to you. Believe that your sensitivity to the needs of others can set in motion a chain of events that will lead to the next Billy Graham. God looks for hearts that are willing, humble, and available. He delights in taking what seems small and filling it with His power. A simple conversation, a quiet act of kindness, a prayer whispered in faith, a helping hand offered at just the right moment - these are the seeds He uses to change lives.

You may not realize how deeply your obedience, compassion, and faithfulness impact those around you, but God does. He weaves His glory through your everyday choices, turning your normal into something supernatural. Never underestimate what God can do through you. You may feel unqualified, unnoticed, or unsure, but God sees potential where you see limitation. He equips those He calls, and He calls those who are willing. Every person you interact with is an opportunity for His love to shine. So walk boldly, love generously, and serve faithfully. Because in God's hands, ordinary becomes extraordinary - and your life becomes a testimony of His amazing power and grace. You are called by God to make a difference in this world. Believe that you can make such an impact on others that potentially millions of people will come to see the light. Jesus said in John 15:16, "You have not chosen Me, but I have chosen you, and ordained you, that you should go and bring forth fruit, and that your fruit should remain."

You have a divine calling on your life to bring forth fruit that will remain and multiply. It is your assignment to impact the world and influence other people. Know this, revival starts with you. Stop making excuses because Jesus said the gates of hell shall not prevail against the church (Matt. 16:18). The end is near and we all must be consumed with a sense of evangelistic urgency. No longer can we put off until tomorrow what we should be doing today. You doing nothing because of a lack of urgency and sensitivity becomes a death sentence to those God would have cross your path. Put off the spirit of slumber and indifference and go out and engage in the lives of other people. Be kind and generous to them and let them know you care. Listen to what people have to say because a hearing ear is one of the surest ways to get people to be willing to hear what you have to say. Deep down people are searching for truth and you must be prepared to give it to them. Learn what they believe and then share the gospel in relation to those beliefs.

Because the gospel message is so powerful, ordinary people like Edward Kimball the shoe salesman can be used to change the world. If you don't like the condition the world is in, then change it. After all, that's why you're here. You're here to change the world and make it a better place. This is both a challenge and a calling. God never placed you on this earth to simply observe darkness, complain about it, or become discouraged by it. He put a spark inside you - His spark - so that you could be the change this world needs. You are not here by accident; you are here on assignment. Whenever God sees a problem on earth, He sends a person. Whenever He sees suffering, He raises up a servant. When He desires transformation, He births a reformer, a leader, a voice of hope. That person is you. The world may be imperfect, but you were created to shine in imperfect places. You carry the light of Christ, and light is not intimidated by darkness - it overcomes it.

Unfortunately, most people can't or won't change by themselves. This is why it takes a leader to bring forth positive change in the world. John Maxwell said, "Change is the indispensable link to turning things around. Change is awkward and a good leader gets people to do what they don't want to do." You may not change the whole world at once, but you can change your world: the people you touch, the atmosphere you carry, the love you show, the truth you speak, the compassion you give, the prayers you release. Don't wait for someone else to rise. Don't wait for conditions to improve. Don't wait for approval or applause. You are the one God has equipped for this moment. If you don't like the way things are then pray, act, serve, speak, love, give, build. Do what God placed in your heart to do. You were never meant to blend into the world; you were meant to transform it. After all, that's why you're here. You're here to change the world and make it a better place.

Because of the awkwardness of change, moat people are more comfortable with old problems than they are with new solutions. This is why if you want to influence people to put off the old and put on the new, you have to plan ahead. You have to predetermine the change that needs to take place. This can only happen by getting close to people and asking them questions. This is how you find out where they are and what changes need to be made. You don't lead from a distance. You lead by getting up close and personal. Their answers to your questions will become the strategy to bring about positive change. The strategy is inside the people, and it takes a sensitive and caring leader to pull it out of them. This is why you need to enter their world. A leader can only lead if they're walking side by side with the people they're trying to influence. If you get too far ahead of them, they'll lose sight of where they need to go. You have to walk beside them so they can participate with you in the journey. You need to be there so you can listen to them and interact with them. After all, you're in this journey together.

Once you know what needs to be done, you can now plan the steps you and the people need to take to bring forth positive change. To begin, you have to adjust your priorities. Sometimes adjustments have to be made. Most times pregame strategies get changed during halftime adjustments. This is why prov. 16:9 says, "A man's heart plans his way, but the Lord directs his steps." We make our plans but ultimately God determines what happens. Knowing that God is with us gives us confidence and the assurance that we will reach our destination no matter what route we take to get there. Also, don't be in too much of a hurry to get to where you're going. Give the people time to accept the changes you tell them have to be made. Intuition and timing is critical if you want to be a good leader. Give people the time they need to gain the confidence required to move forward with you. Yes, you're eager to press forward and move on but sometimes you have to slow down until the people get the same enthusiasm you have.

Most leaders are wired for speed. They see the destination long before others even notice the road. Vision burns in their hearts, passion drives their steps, and momentum becomes a way of life. But there is a holy wisdom every leader must learn: If you never slow down, you will eventually get too far ahead of the people you're called to lead - and that's not leadership anymore. Jesus moved with purpose, yet He also moved paced Himself. He never rushed past the needs of the people. He walked with His disciples, not miles ahead of them. He taught them, waited for them, corrected them, and carried them when necessary. His power was great, but His patience was greater. Time and effort are needed to make clear to the people what's taking place and what they need to do. People will not follow what they do not understand. Leaders understand the value of clarity when communicating with people. Take the time to talk to people and answer their questions until they fully understand what you expect them to do.

Progress without people is not kingdom success. Speed without shepherding is not spiritual leadership. Sometimes the most anointed thing you can do is slow down long enough to listen, to teach again, to explain patiently, to walk beside someone who's struggling to keep up. If you run too far ahead, you'll look back and realize you're alone. But if you match your pace with God's timing and the people's capacity, you'll not only reach the destination, you'll also arrive together, stronger, wiser, and unified. So lead with vision but walk with grace. Move with purpose but stay close enough to guide. Because leadership is not measured by how fast you move but by how many people you bring with you. Leaders understand that progress means little if others are left behind in the shadows of their success. A spiritual leader slows down when necessary, reaches back with grace, and says, "Let's walk this out together." In God's Kingdom, speed is never the measure of greatness, but stewardship, compassion, and responsibility are.

A good leader knows the way, goes the way, and shows the way. The key is to become the type of leader people love to follow. To make a positive impact you must be a person who is respected and admired, a person who it would be an honor to follow. This happens when you give the people a vision for a better life. You stand with them and help them do what needs to be done. Along the way you give them positive feedback and sound advice of how to make their life better. This will show that you love them, you trust them, and you believe in them. People will be open to your influence and leadership when you make them feel empowered, loved, valued, and trusted. Your goal is not to become a leader everyone loves but a leader everyone loves to follow. There is a big difference between a leader who is popular and one who is respected. As a leader, you may be popular if you are respected, but you will never be respected if you are only trying to be popular.

People will respect you and follow you when you make them feel valued, when they know you really, truly do care about them. Your leadership needs to inspire people. You need to breathe life into them and fill them with the urge to do things they've never done before. This, in turn, will make them feel empowered. You have given them the confidence to take that first step to a better life. A good leader creates an environment where the people feel valued, inspired, and empowered. To do this you must have a heart that cares about people. You will never be a leader others love to follow if you aren't a leader who genuinely loves people. Maya Angelo said, "People will forget what you said. People will forget what you did. But people will never forget how you made them feel." People need to know that they truly matter to you. Look these people in the eye and say, "I notice what you do and what you do matters to me."

People get greatly discouraged when they do good things and nobody notices. Your calling is to tell these people you notice and appreciate what they do. Embrace the need to tell people how much you appreciate them. This will make them feel valued and cause them to follow wherever you feel led to take them. Celebrate the good people do. Never rob the people you're trying to influence of the blessing of knowing that you notice what they do and that you care. Let people know they're here for a God-given purpose. Let they know their life matters and the world got better the day they were born. The best leaders help people see how special and important they are. You need to have a passion that inspires people, to pull out of them the good things already inside of them. Being generous with recognition is inspirational. When you tell people how incredible they are you'll grab their attention, and they'll be open to your positive influence.

To be a leader that people love to follow, you must be a person who glows in the dark. Like Jesus, be a light in the tunnel people are passing through. Jesus had a caring heart and He loved to mingle with the worst of the worst, the lowest of the low, people whom society had rejected. He loved to befriend sinners, people who were hurting, people who were broken, prostitutes, tax collectors, those who were despised in their day. He would reach out to those that religion rejected and He would care about them and show them love, grace, and mercy. He came to inspire people. He would say, "It's not about Me. I didn't come to be served but I came to serve others. I came to serve you." He said, "I have come that you may have life, and that you may have it more abundantly, a better life than you ever dreamed of."

Because of His sacrificial leadership He was a man people loved to follow. He cared for people, valued them, inspired them, and empowered them. You need to do the same thing if you want people to follow you.

| 8 |

"SEEDS OF BLESSING"

You were put on this earth to make a contribution. Eph. 2:10 (TEV) says, "God has created us for a life of good deeds, which He has already prepared for us to do." In fact, your loving service to others shows you are truly saved. 1 John 3:14 (CEV), "Our love for each other proves that we have gone from death to life." You were not placed on this earth by accident. Before you ever took your first breath, God wrote a purpose over your life - a special assignment designed uniquely for you. You carry gifts, experiences, and a calling that no one else can fulfill in the exact way you can. Heaven entrusted you with a mission that has your fingerprints on it. And when Christ saves a heart, He also reshapes it. A saved heart is a serving heart, one that wants to serve others and help make their lives better. It feels the quiet nudge to reach out, to lift up, to encourage, to help someone else find their way. And each time you serve, you reflect the heart of the One who served you first.

Wake up each morning with the question, "Lord, whose needs can I meet today?" No matter what your past was like or your background, God can and will use you. Consider how God used Abraham who was old, Jacob was insecure, Leah was unattractive, Joseph was abused, Gideon was poor, and Rahab was immoral. Consider also David who committed adultery and murder, Elijah was suicidal, Jeremiah was depressed, Jonah was reluctant, and Naomi was a widow. Then again there's the impulsive and hot-tempered Peter, Martha worried a lot, Zacchaeus was unpopular, Thomas had doubts, and Timothy was timid. All of these people were far from perfect, but God used each and every one of them for His service. If He used them, He can use you also. Know and believe that God designed you to make a difference with your life. He made you to be salt and light, to be an extension of Himself in this world. You are here on purpose. You are chosen for a reason. You are equipped for your assignment.

Salvation doesn't just change your destiny - it changes your desires. It awakens compassion, deepens love, and stirs a longing to make someone's life better, even in small, unseen ways. Your assignment may not always look grand or dramatic. Sometimes it's a simple word of kindness, a prayer for someone who's struggling, a small act of generosity that feels insignificant to you but means everything to them. Other times, God will call you to step out boldly and shine His love in places that desperately need light. Jude 22 says, "And on some have compassion, making a difference." Let that be your mission statement, the assignment you've been called to fulfill. Jude tells us that it is love and compassion that causes us to make a difference in the world. In other words, you need to live a life marked by generosity. Our God is a kind, loving, compassionate God. Living generously begins with the recognition that our God is a generous God, the model and example of the life we've been called to live.

Ps. 100:5 says, "For God is sheer beauty, all-generous in love, loyal always and forever." Rom. 10:13 (MSG), "Everyone who calls, 'Help, God!' gets help." Ps. 63:3 says, "In Your generous love I am really living at last!" Live a life marked by generosity. Give to others the things they need. Deut. 15:10 says, "Give freely and spontaneously. Don't have a stingy heart." Differences are made by compassion, by love that is real. God is love and you are too. You will impact the world when love rules supreme in your life. Deut. 15:11 says, "So I command you: Always be generous, open purse and hand, give to your neighbors in trouble, your poor and hurting neighbors." Generous people make an impact on this world. A person who does "not grow weary in doing good" (Gal. 6:9) lives a life that leads to increased effectiveness. A person with a generous heart has a deep desire to help others. They're open-minded and are always thinking of ways to help people during their time of need.

Plan to be a blessing to others. Is. 32:8 says, "A generous man devises generous plans, and by generosity he shall stand." All the fulfillment of life comes from helping others to expand and exceed their worth on this planet, to become more than what they could become on their own. Help people every day. Bless them, lift them up, add value to their life. tell them how special they are and how honored you are to be their friend. You're here to serve people. Benjamin Franklin once said, "No one is useless in this world who lightens the burden of someone else." Make it your lifestyle to giving people whatever it is they need. 1 Tim. 6:18 says "to do good, to be rich in helping others, to be extravagantly generous." If you want to become the type of person God can use anytime and anywhere, then offer yourself continually to the service of others. A willing heart in the hands of the Lord becomes a powerful instrument for His purposes.

When you make yourself ready to serve, heaven takes notice. When you choose compassion over convenience and people over comfort, God shapes you into someone He can trust with His assignments. Serving others is not a task reserved for certain moments - it is a posture of the heart. It is waking up each day and saying, "Lord, here I am. Use me today." It means carrying the love of Christ into ordinary places, speaking life where there is discouragement, offering help where there is need, and showing kindness where there is hurt. Every act of service, whether big or small, becomes a seed God uses to change lives - including your own. Service softens the heart, strengthens character, removes selfishness, and tunes your spirit to God's voice. It positions you under God's hand so that when He calls, you are already in motion. If you truly desire to be used by God, don't wait for a platform, a title, or a microphone. Look for the person in front of you. Listen for the cry of the hurting. Pay attention to the silent burdens people carry.

When your life becomes a vessel of service, God will use you anytime, anywhere. Not because you are perfect, but because you are willing. Mahatma Gandhi said, "The best way to find yourself is to lose yourself in the service of others." Every day go out into the world and lose yourself. Be the type of person who says "yes" to every request made of you. Whatever the need may be, always say, "Yes, I will help meet that need." Albert Schweitzer said, "I don't know what your destiny will be but one thing I know: the ones among you who will be really happy are those who have sought and found how to serve." Sow seeds of blessing wherever you go. Give your life away daily. Jesus said in Luke 6:38 (MSG), "Giving, not getting, is the way. Generosity begets generosity." John Maxwell said, "The happiest people in life are not always the most successful people but they are the ones who serve the best." Greatness in the kingdom of God comes in our service to others. Martin Luther King Jr. once said, "Everybody can be great because everybody can serve."

Only one time in scripture did Jesus say, "Follow Me and follow My example." That was when He was washing the feet of the disciples and serving them. Good leadership is not about getting people to join your team. It's about serving people and doing what's best for them. True leaders are motivated by loving concern rather than personal glory. It's not about what people can do for you, it's about what you can do for them. A servant puts service over status. To impact the world, you've got to forget about yourself. Life isn't about what you can get, it's about what you can give. Also, a servant puts character over comfort. In other words, they do the right thing whether they feel like doing it or not. By living generously, you'll attract people to God. Jesus said, "Be generous with your lives. By opening up to others, you'll prompt people to open up with God" (Matt. 5:14). When you love people and value them, you'll make people hungry for God. Sometimes, a simple act of kindness is all the influence people need.

By blessing others, you'll live out your God-created identity. Never are you more like Jesus than when you spend your life to help make the lives of other people better. God has never created anything without a purpose, without a meaning. From the smallest flower to the vast heavens above, everything exists by His intentional design. Nothing in creation is accidental, and nothing is without purpose. If God put it here, He put it here for a reason. The very fact that you are alive proves that there is a purpose for your life. You are not a mistake. You are not an afterthought. Before you ever took your first breath, God had already spoken destiny over your life. Scripture says, "Before I formed you in the womb, I knew you" (Jer. 1:5). This means your purpose preceded your existence. God crafted you with intention, shaped you with care, and breathed life into you because there is something you were uniquely designed to accomplish. Even when life feels confusing, chaotic, or ordinary, heaven still sees purpose written all over you.

Walk boldly in the truth that your life is overflowing with divine purpose. You matter to God, and you matter to this world. You are here on purpose and for a purpose. The greatest adventure in life is being used by God to fulfill the purpose for which you were created. Indeed, there is no greater thrill than that. God smiles when He sees you doing what you've been called to do. But know this, God uses you only if and when you are usable. God uses you only when you're willing to be used. And to be used, you must be prepared to be used. You must be ready when the call comes to take action. Jesus said in Luke 12:35 (NLT), "Be dressed for service and well prepared." He is saying you must be ready to be used by God and to experience His power in your life. How do you get ready to be used by God? First, you must purify your heart. Your motivation to do anything is based on the condition of your heart. Get the sin and garbage out of your life. Saint Augustine once said, "The confession of bad works is the beginning of good works."

Job 11:13-16 (NLT), "Prepare your heart and lift up your hands to Him in prayer! Get rid of your sins and leave all iniquity behind you. Then your face will brighten in innocence. You'll be strong and free of fear. You will forget your misery. It will all be gone like water under the bridge." Joshua said to the people in Josh.3:5, "Purify yourselves, for tomorrow the Lord will do great wonders among you." To be set apart for the purposes of God for your life, you must be willing to separate yourself from all things that might defile you. 2 Tim. 2:21 (NLT), "If you keep yourself pure, you will be a special utensil for honorable use. Your life will be clean, and you will be ready for the Master to use you for every good work." God wants to use you to do great things but first you have to purify your heart. Confess your sins to God and He'll cleanse you from all unrighteousness (1 John 1:9). We all miss the mark from time to time but there is no excuse for willful, habitual sin.

Keep yourself pure and God will use you for His purpose. There is a sacred power in honesty before God. When you confess your sins, you are not informing God of something He doesn't already know - you are agreeing with Him about what has been holding you back. Confession opens the door for cleansing, for restoration, and for freedom. But confession is only the beginning. True repentance means turning your back on the sin and walking away from it. When you step out of the shadows and into God's light, the guilt loses its grip, the shame loses its voice, and the enemy loses his leverage. As you lay your sin at the feet of Jesus and choose to walk in a new direction, something beautiful happens - your life becomes clean. Your heart becomes clear. Your spirit becomes available. God delights in using clean vessels. He pours His power, His wisdom, and His anointing into those who have allowed Him to clean the inside first. When you confess and walk away from sin, you become someone God can trust with deeper assignments, greater influence, and stronger spiritual authority.

Once you purify your heart, you must then sanctify your body. The word "sanctify" means 'to dedicate for a special purpose.' Rom. 6:13 (NLT), "Give yourselves completely to God and use your whole body as a tool to do what is right for the glory of God." The Message Bible says, "Throw yourselves wholeheartedly and fulltime into God's way of doing things." 1 Cor. 6:20 (MSG) says your body was "made for God-given and God-modeled love. So let people see God in and through your body." There comes a point in every believer's journey when halfway surrender simply will not do. God is not looking for partial devotion, occasional obedience, or convenient faith. He is calling us to a life fully yielded, a heart, mind, and body placed entirely in His hands. To give yourself completely to God means you stop holding back the parts of your life you've kept guarded, things such as your plans, your desires, your habits, your comforts. It means trusting Him enough to say, "Lord, all that I am and all that I have is Yours."

Scripture tells us to offer our whole body as a tool for righteousness. Let your hands be used to help and heal. Let your feet walk toward places where God needs you. Let your eyes look upon things that honor Him. Let your mouth speak life, truth, and encouragement. Let your mind be filled with His Word and guided by His Spirit. When your whole being becomes an instrument in God's hands, your life becomes a living testimony of His glory. People no longer simply hear the gospel from you - they see it in how you move, how you love, how you serve, and how you stand firm. This kind of surrender isn't bondage; it's freedom from the weight of trying to direct your own life, freedom from sin's grip, and freedom to live out the purpose God designed for you. The more you give yourself to Him, the more He fills you with strength, peace, and joy. Place your whole life before Him and say, "Lord, use my body, my voice, my energy, my gifts - everything - for Your glory." When God has all of you, He can do more through you than you ever imagined.

To get ready to be used by God, you must simplify your schedule. Don't fall into the trap of being too busy to be used for the Master's work. A life that is too busy, cluttered, or distracted cannot fully hear His voice or respond to His call. Jesus often withdrew from the crowds to pray, to rest, and to focus on His mission. If He needed that, how much more do we? God gives you enough time to do His will. If, for some reason, you don't have enough time, then there are some things you shouldn't be doing. Simplifying your schedule is not about doing less; it's about prioritizing what truly matters. It's saying no to the urgent things that do not advance God's kingdom so you can say yes to the opportunities He places before you. It's creating quiet moments to listen, reflect, and respond to His guidance. Do not fall into the trap of busyness. Being constantly occupied may feel productive, but it can blind you to God's appointments, His assignments, and His purpose. A life simplified becomes a life available for the Master to use.

The problem is God has a plan for your life and so does everyone else. They want you to spend on them the time you should be spending fulfilling God's purposes. Learn to say "no" to people who would rob you of your time to serve God. Titus 2:12 says the grace of God "teaches us to say no to ungodliness and worldly passions." Saying "no" to time thieves allows you to stay focused on what God wants you to do instead of what everyone else wants you to do. Ask yourself, "What can I release today so I have space for God to move? What distractions can I remove so His work in me and through me is not hindered?" The simpler your life, the greater your availability and the more powerfully God can work through you. Let go of distractions, unclutter your heart, and watch how powerfully He can move through you. A simple life isn't empty - it's available. The quieter your soul, the louder God's love can shine through you. Less noise, more God.

Eph. 5:16 says we should be "redeeming the time because the days are evil." The NLT says, "Make the most of every opportunity for doing good in these evil days." Time is one of the most precious gifts God has given us. Each moment is a seed of potential, an opportunity to walk in purpose, love, and faith. Yet too often we allow our days to be consumed by fleeting pleasures, distractions, or pursuits that leave no lasting mark on the world. The Bible says in Ps. 90:12, "Teach us to number our days, that we may gain a heart of wisdom." Wisdom comes when we recognize that our time is limited and choose to invest it in what truly matters: serving others, building godly character, growing in faith, and making an eternal impact. We can't waste our time on fleshly pursuits that leave no impact on the world. Titus 3:8 says, "All who trust in God will devote themselves to doing good." Make plans that align with God's will. The Message Bible says, "Concentrate on the essentials that are good for everyone."

Jesus said in John 9:4 (NLT), "We must quickly carry out the tasks assigned to us by the One who sent us." He then said, "Night is coming when no one can work." Jesus was diligent about keeping to His mission. He redeemed the time and changed the world forever. Discipline is not a restriction - it is stewardship. Just as a master gardener tends carefully to his garden, so we must tend to our days with intention. Every hour spent in prayer, in acts of love, in learning, or in fulfilling our calling is a treasure that bears fruit far beyond the present moment. Do not let time slip away chasing what is temporary. Live with purpose, act with intention, and let every moment honor God. Time is one of the most precious gifts God gives us. Every moment we are alive is an opportunity to honor Him - not just with words, but with the way we live. How we spend our hours, our days, and our seasons reflects the heart we offer to the Giver of life.

| 9 |

"A LEGACY OF GENEROSITY"

To be put in a position where you can impact the world, you must intensify your passion for God. Why? Because He only uses people who are passionate for Him. You can't be a casual, part-time Christian and be used by God. You must be sold out for God and for His plan and purpose on the earth. Tell Him with all sincerity that you want to be the person He wants you to be, that you want to live the life you were created to live. Go all in with your relationship with God. Hold nothing back in your effort to please Him and be used by Him. The truth is, He only uses those who want it the most. The desire to serve God and impact the world should be the strongest craving you have. Let your light shine with high intensity. Let people see your good works and they'll glorify your Father who is in heaven (Matt. 5:16). Charles Spurgeon said, "I would not give much for your religion unless it can be seen. Lamps do not talk but they do shine."

Live in such a way that your light radiates brilliantly for all to see. To shine is not optional. A failure to shine is a failure to fulfill your heavenly call. The greatest definition of "success" is found in what Jesus said in John 17:4, "I have brought You glory on earth by completing the work You gave Me to do." Good intentions mean little if they're not backed up with action. Go out and impact the world. "Be doers of the word and not hearers only" (James 1:22). To impact the world, you must live a generous life. You can be generous with your thoughts, words, money, influence, time, attention, and belongings. What is generosity? It's the taking of your entire life, everything you are and everything you have, and using it to bless people around you. In order to make a positive difference in the world you need to keep your antenna up. You must be aware of the needs of those you come in contact with.

When you're sensitive to the needs of others you'll have the opportunity to create a legacy of generosity, a legacy that will impact people long after you're gone. Sometimes when the things you do seem insignificant at the moment is the very thing that ushers in the power of God to do miraculous things. Life is a journey and God wants you to be a purpose driven person. He wants you to pursue and be driven by His plan and His purpose for your life. Life is too short to be wasted. The God-kind of life in not measured in its duration but in its donation, in the things you do to bless our generation. Because life is short, it is critical that you be intentional in how you live. Make it your aim to make a maximum impact in life and to leave a lasting legacy. You are the salt of the earth and the light of the world, and you've been called to make this world a better place. Living a life of positive impact is indeed possible. All you have to do is believe that God can and will use you.

Jesus "emptied Himself" (Phil. 2:7) to bless us, so must we empty ourselves to bless others. That is what living a generous life is all about. Helping others live a better life should be the very core of our existence. Jesus gave everything He had, and you need to do the same thing. Grace is when God gives us more than we deserve. Likewise, living a generous life is when we give others more than they deserve. Christian hospitality encompasses an attitude of openness, kindness, and a willingness to serve others. Keep doing good things until your generosity grabs the world's attention. By being generous to people you'll create opportunities to share your faith, to demonstrate God's love, and to invite others into a relationship with Christ. Through generosity you'll have the privilege of blessing and positively impacting the lives of others, both materially and spiritually.

Jesus demonstrated hospitality by engaging in a conversation with a Samaritan woman at a well. He showed her kindness, respect, and a genuine concern for her life (John 4:4-26). The early church shared their possessions and resources with one another. They provided for the needs of those in their midst (Acts 2:42-47; Acts 4:32-37). Lydia extended hospitality to Paul and his companions in Philippi. She invited them to stay in her house and eventually got saved and baptized (Acts 16:11-15). Dorcas was known for her acts of kindness and charity. She made clothing for the needy and showed hospitality through her service to others (Acts 9:36-42). Consider Abraham who demonstrated exceptional hospitality when he welcomed three strangers into his tent. He provided them with food, water, and a place to rest (Gen. 18:1-15). This act of kindness turned out to be a divine encounter as two of the visitors were angels who delivered important messages and blessings to Abraham and his wife Sarah.

Every child of God has the responsibility to love God whole-heartedly, love others sacrificially, and make disciples for His kingdom (Luke 10:27,28). Josh. 2:1-21 tells how Rahab the harlot showed hospitality and protected two Israelite spies who came to scout out the city she lived in. She hid them on her rooftop and helped them escape from the authorities. Jesus demonstrated hospitality by reaching out to Zacchaeus, a tax collector and social outcast, and inviting Himself to his home (Luke 19:1-10). This act of kindness, this act of acceptance and fellowship, led to Zacchaeus's divine transformation and commitment to restitution. In the parable of the Good Samaritan, Jesus taught about the importance of showing compassion and hospitality to those in need, even those from different backgrounds (Luke 10:25-37). The Jews at that time wanted nothing to do with those from Samaria but this good Samaritan cared for a wounded stranger, exemplifying the command to love your neighbor.

Hospitality is far more than an act of kindness - it is a sacred doorway through which God's love enters the world. When you open your heart and your home to others, you are doing more than meeting a need; you are creating space for heaven to touch earth. By practicing hospitality, you not only extend a helping hand, but you also create opportunities for divine encounters, spiritual growth, and the strengthening of community bonds. Every time you welcome someone with compassion, you become a vessel of God's grace. Moments of fellowship can turn into revelations. Simple conversations can become life changing. A shared meal can become a moment where burdens lift, hope rises, and hearts heal. In showing love to others, you reflect the very heart of Christ who welcomed the weary, the broken, and the searching. Your open door may be the very place where someone encounters God's presence for the first time and where you encounter Him in a brand-new way.

Christian hospitality that is deeply rooted in the teachings of the Bible exemplifies the heart of Christ's message and His call to love and serve others. Open your home to newcomers, visitors, or people in need. Invite them for a meal, provide for them a place to stay, or simply offer a listening ear. Share your material resources with others. This could include providing food, clothing, or financial assistance to those facing difficulties. Look for opportunities to connect with people overlooked by society, such as the lonely, the homeless, the elderly, or those from different cultural backgrounds. Engage in meaningful conversations that show genuine interest in people's lives, experience, and needs. Do this and people will surely open up to you. Encourage them to invite God into their situation. Offer prayers and emotional support for those going through challenging times, expressing genuine concern and care. God has called you to stand beside the weary, to lift up the brokenhearted, and to intercede for those who feel too weak to pray for themselves.

Show hospitality in everyday situations. Practice small acts of kindness, such as giving a compliment, holding the door for someone, helping with a task that needs to be done. Perform acts of service for others, such as volunteering at a shelter, offering rides to those in need, mowing the lawn for an elderly neighbor. Create a welcoming environment. Make your home a place where people feel comfortable and accepted, fostering a sense of belonging. And never forget what Jesus said in Matt. 25:40 (NIV), "Whatever you did for one of the least of these brothers and sisters of Mine, you did for Me." The virtue of being hospitable is that you are a lover of what is beneficial to others. You are generous when it comes to helping those in need. Is. 58:7 tells you "to share your food with the hungry and to bring to your home the poor who are cast out. When you see the naked, that you cover him."

A person who is hospitable must be a lover of strangers, must enjoy having guests in his home, must always be ready to help others. Biblical hospitality is a sacred duty to treat strangers and friends alike, welcoming one another into our homes and into our very lives. In Rom. 12:13, Paul uses hospitality as a defining mark of a Christian when he writes, "Share with the saints in their needs, pursue hospitality." The NLT says, "Always be eager to practice hospitality" and the Message Bible says, "Help needy Christians, be inventive in hospitality." Every child of God should be eager for opportunities to show hospitality to others. Gal. 6:10 says, "As we have opportunity, let us do good to all." This involves more than a pat on the back and a handshake. It's about sharing the burdens and blessings of others so that we all grow together and glorify the

Lord. Bible commentator John Murray said, "We are to iden-tify ourselves with the needs of others and make them our own."

Make their needs your needs to the full extent of your ability to relieve them. After all, 1 Cor. 12:26 says, "If one member suffers, all the members suffer with them." Paul says to pursue hospitality. Actively go out and look for ways to bless people. Put some effort into it. Seek and you shall find. Paul is speaking of an intensity of effort which leads to a pursuit with earnest-ness and diligence in order to lay hold of what you're pur-suing. God never called us to be passive observers of His goodness - He called us to be active vessels of it. Each day carries new opportunities to bless someone, but those oppor-tunities often reveal themselves only to the ones who are look-ing for them. Don't wait for someone to stumble into your kindness; go out intentionally and search for moments to lift, help, and encourage. So step out today with a heart awake and a spirit ready. Ask God to guide your steps, sharpen your awareness, and use you as a blessing wherever you go. Some-one's breakthrough, comfort, or hope may be waiting on the other side of your obedience.

Hospitality plays no small role in the realm of biblical ethics. It must be literally chased after like one hunts an animal and delights to carry the plunder home. Press hard in your effort to show kindness to others. Put effort into blessing others be-cause effort is evidence of love. When you open your eyes with purpose, you'll begin to see needs you once overlooked and hearts you can touch with just a word, a gesture, or a prayer. Remember, the hands and feet of Christ don't stand still. They move, they reach, they act. William Barclay said, "Christianity is the religion of the open hand, the open heart, and the open door." Heb. 13:1 says, "Let brotherly love continue." Pursuing hospitality is to be a God-empowered lifestyle and habitual practice to diligently go out and show love and kindness to others. God's people must always be ready to practice hospitality to those in need, whether it be family, close friends, or people they have never seen before.

1 Peter 4:8,9 (MSG) says, "Love makes up for practically anything. Be generous with the different things God gave you, passing them around so all get in on it." To make an impact on the world you must be given to the generous and cordial reception of guests, offering them a pleasant and sustaining environment to be in. You must understand that hospitality is a command. It's something you're told to do. Heb. 13:2 (NLT) says, "Don't forget to show hospitality to strangers." This simple instruction carries the heartbeat of God. Hospitality is more than offering a meal or a place to sit - it is opening the door of your heart. It is looking beyond your own circle and making room for someone who has nothing to offer you in return. You never know who is standing in front of you. The person you greet, the one you smile at, the one you show kindness to, may be carrying a burden you cannot see. Your gentle word, your generosity, or your act of compassion may be the very touch of God they have been praying for.

Heaven pays attention to how we treat those who cannot do anything for us. God is honored when His people open their lives to the overlooked, the outcast, and the unknown. Heb. 13:1,2 (MSG), "Stay on good terms with each other, held together by love. Be ready with a meal or a bed when it's needed." So be intentional. Slow down. Notice the ones others walk past. Offer kindness freely. Extend grace joyfully. Let your home, your schedule, and your heart be a place where strangers can find warmth, dignity, and love. Because when you show hospitality to others, you are welcoming God's presence into your own life. We should all approach the practice of biblical hospitality with joy and happiness. It's something we should look forward to doing each and every day. 2 Cor. 9:7 says, "Each of you should give what you have decided in your heart to give, not reluctantly or under compulsion, for God loves a cheerful giver." An unselfish person is generous in every area of their life. They're generous with their time, their energy, their praise, their talents, and their treasure.

Why is generosity so important? Because it is love in action. You can give without loving but you can't love without giving. You can't be loving without being generous. Giving can be done out of duty, habit, or even for appearance but love is different. Love cannot stay still. Love moves. Love reaches. Love pours itself out for the good of another. True love is always expressed through giving, not only in material ways, but in patience, kindness, compassion, prayer, and service. When the love of God fills your heart, it becomes impossible to stay closed, cold, or distant. Love makes you generous with forgiveness. It makes you generous with encouragement. It makes you generous with your time, your attention, your words, and your resources. Love transforms giving from an obligation into a joyful expression of who you are in Christ. Let your giving flow from a heart that loves like Jesus. Because when love is real, giving becomes natural. It becomes joyful. It becomes worship. Love gives... always.

In the Bible, the word "believe" is used 272 times, the word "pray" is used 371 times, and word "love" is used 714 times, and the word "give" is used 2152 times. Why should you be generous? First and foremost, it honors God. 2 Cor. 9:13 (NLT) says, "You will be glorifying God through your generous gifts." Prov. 14:31 (ESV) says, "Whoever is generous to the needy honors God." Know always that God is honored each and every time you bless those who cross your path. He sees it all whether it's a word of encouragement, a small act of kindness, a prayer whispered in someone's moment of need, or a helping hand extended in compassion. Second, generosity expands your influence in the world. The more generous you are, the more influential you will become. Yes, influence comes from generosity. Prov. 11:24 (MSG) says, "The world of the generous gets larger and larger; the world of the stingy will get smaller and smaller." Ps. 112:9 (NLT) says, "Those who give generously to those in need will never be forgotten. They will have influence and honor."

Biblical hospitality is not merely a work of our hands but involves a work in our hearts. We must love people from the inside out. People know when love is real and genuine. They'll know it when they see it. Love is expressed in generous actions and not merely in words. Open your life to others with no barriers. Make yourself readily accessible to those in need, forever ready to lend a helping hand. When you welcome someone into your heart and home, treat them like they belong. Why? Because in the kingdom of God they do belong. Let's face it, in the world isolation, brokenness, and loneliness are all too common. This is why the men of God need to step up and practice hospitality daily. Welcome these people with open arms and see them as uniquely created in God's image. Respond to their needs with loving care and generosity. Theologian Scott Cormode said, "Hospitality is an offer to identify with outsiders and to treat them like insiders."

Hospitality is the offer to extend the privileges of community to those who feel left out and vulnerable because they are strangers. Croatian theologian Miroslav Volf said, "Having been embraced by God, we must make space for others and invite them in, even our enemies." Lev. 19:34 says, "But the stranger who dwells among you shall be to you as one born among you, and you shall love him as yourself." Luke 9 is an interesting passage for understanding what Jesus was trying to teach the disciples about hospitality. At the beginning of the chapter, Jesus sends out the twelve disciples without provisions. He purposely asks them to rely on the hospitality of others. Why did Jesus do this? Because He knew there was no better way to understand the people entrusted to your care than to have you walk in their shoes and to live on their terms. Jesus intentionally put the powerful gospel message in the hands of powerless people. He then made them dependent on the kindness of other people.

Hospitality is often the first experience outsiders have with God's people and the loving God they represent. They measure their acceptance by our hospitality toward them. Rom. 15:7 (AMP) says, "Welcome and receive one another, then, even as Christ has welcomed and received you, for the glory of God." Paul commands us to continually make hospitality our lifestyle. We are to be supernatural "acceptors" of those we come in contact with. "Reach out and welcome one another to God's glory" (MSG). Give people a warm welcome. Treat them as the closest of friends with the most caring kindness. "Let your love be without hypocrisy" (Rom. 12:9). Let the love of God flow out from inside of you and demonstrate a genuine heartfelt acceptance of others. Both globally and locally there is a desperate need for a fresh obedience to this often-neglected biblical command. Begin today the journey of hospitality.

| 10 |

"A GIFT FROM GOD"

Let's face it, life is passing by at a rapid pace. Like the blink of an eye the years keep going by faster than a lightning strike. In the midst of this hectic world, we have to put on the brakes and ask ourselves, "Are we making our lives count?' Are we listening to the voice of God? Are we responding to the things He's telling us to do? Are we actively trying to make this world a better place? There are people everywhere striving for your attention and the last thing you want to do is say you're too busy to help them. In a world filled with noise, distractions, and endless responsibilities, it's easy to rush past the very people God has placed in your path. But every knock on your door, every voice calling your name, every moment where someone reaches for your attention may be a divine appointment - an opportunity to reveal God's love through simple acts of kindness. You don't have to solve every problem - you simply need to make yourself available.

Jesus Himself was often pressed by crowds, surrounded by needs, and approached at inconvenient moments. Yet He never said, *"I'm too busy."* He paused for the woman with the issue of blood, He turned to listen to blind Bartimaeus, He stopped under a sycamore tree for Zacchaeus. His schedule never outweighed His compassion. You mirror the heart of Christ when you slow down long enough to notice the people around you. Your smile, your listening ear, your prayer, your encouragement may be exactly what someone needs to keep going. You don't have to solve every problem - you simply need to make yourself available. There are hurting people all over your community who need you to make an impact on their life, to give them the help they so desperately need. So be intentional and look around you. Allow God to interrupt your plans. Let love guide your steps. Because sometimes the greatest ministry happens in the moments you didn't plan for.

Stop striving for worldly success that will never satisfy your inner cravings for meaning and purpose. No matter how high you climb or how much you accumulate, it will never silence the deeper cry within you. There is a longing in every soul that no achievement, applause, or earthly reward can ever satisfy. That hunger is not a flaw; it is a divine signal pointing you back to your true purpose. You need to slow down and fulfill the call of God on your life. You were not created to impress people - you were created to impact eternity. Success without God leaves you empty, but surrender to His plan fills you with peace, direction, and meaning. Lay down the constant striving. Release the pressure to perform. Step out of the rat race and into the rest of God. Slow down. Listen. Obey. When you choose God's purpose over the world's expectations, you don't lose anything - you find everything. Why? Because true success is not measured by what you build with your hands, but by what God builds within you.

Your life's deepest fulfillment will be found not in chasing the world, but in answering the call of God on your life. Rom. 8:28, "We know that in all things God works for the good of those who love Him, who have been called according to His purpose." Your calling and God's purpose go together. They're one and the same. 2 Tim. 1:9 says God "called us with a holy calling according to His own purpose." God's goal for your life is greater than comfort, convenience, or the approval of people. His desire is that you become consumed - fully overtaken - by the call He has placed on your life. Before you were formed in the womb, Heaven spoke your purpose. God breathed destiny into your spirit, and He has never forgotten what He declared over you. His call is not casual; it is divine. It is not random; it is intentional. And it will not be satisfied until you walk in the very thing He created you to do. Your assignment from on high is to live out your calling and let nothing stop you from fulfilling what God has called you to do.

To impact the world, you've got to live out your heavenly calling. This is the only way to find true success in the world, success as God sees it. When you live out your calling, you live from a higher realm, from a place where obedience is your fuel, faith is your compass, and God's voice becomes the loudest sound in your life. Distractions will come. Opposition will rise. People may not understand. But nothing has the authority to stop a person who is surrendered to their assignment from on high. Let the fire of God's purpose burn in you until it shapes how you think, how you act, and how you make decisions. Let the call of God become your passion, your focus, and your pursuit. Shake off every weight. Silence every doubt. Reject every excuse. You were born with a heavenly assignment. Now rise up and fulfill it. God is with you, God is in you, and God has already gone before you. Walk boldly in what He has called you to do and let nothing stop you.

God has a great and eternal plan that He is working out in your life. Don't be like Jonah who ran away when he found out what God wanted him to do. Instead, run toward that plan with vigor and forceful energy. Cling to the call and with great enthusiasm be anxious to impact your world. Yes, there is a heavenly call on every person's life. Your mission is to spend the rest of your life doing what God wants you to do. Eph. 1:18 (CEV) says, "My prayer is that light will flood your hearts and that you will understand the hope that was given to you when God called you." The Message Bible says God wants "your eyes focused and clear, so that you can see exactly what it is He is calling you to do." God wants you to "grasp the immensity of this glorious way of life He has for His followers, oh, the extravagance of His work in us who trust Him" (vs. 19 MSG). When you decide to aggressively work toward the fulfillment of your heavenly call you will be filled with hope knowing that God is committed to your success.

God is on your side and all you have to do is obey Him and do what He tells you to do. When you follow godly direction, when you're led by the Spirit, you are sure to succeed. You can and will impact the world you live in. You will see things differently when you realize that your calling is a gift from God. He wanted to bless you, so He gave you something to do for Him. God has a plan for all of mankind and His present to you is to be a part of that plan. In other words, you are called for God's purposes. He wants you to join Him and be His lifelong partner. You're not here to fulfill your will, you're here to fulfill God's will. Jesus had the same calling. He said to the Father, "Not My will, but Yours be done" (Luke 22:42). God did not create you to live a selfish life, He created you and called you to pour your life into the lives of others. This is how you impact the world. You were made by God to be used for God. Until you understand that life will never make sense. You'll always be asking the question, "Why am I here?"

Like signing your name on a blank check, tell God, "I don't care what it is, I'll do whatever you want me to do. Here I am, send me!" For sure, God will take you up on your offer to serve Him. Before long you'll be influencing people to live a better life. You'll be making an impact on the world. God made you to serve Him. Eph. 2:10 says, "For we are God's workmanship, created in Christ Jesus to do good works, which God prepared in advance for us to do." MSG, "He creates each of us by Christ Jesus to join Him in the work He does, the good work He has gotten ready for us to do, work we had better be doing." God wants you to partner with Him in impacting the world. 1 Cor. 3:9 (GNT) says, "For we are partners working together for God." The NIV says, "We are co-laborers in God's service." We should all strive to become vessels through whom God works. He doesn't use everybody but only those who have surrendered their lives to His will and purpose.

As long as your heart is beating, you have just one purpose in life. You're here to be a surrendered vessel through whom God can do His work. 1 Cor. 6:29 says, "You were bought with a price." Understand that you are not your own. You are God's possession and you're to live according to His will and purposes. A surrendered vessel has been cleansed of all selfish desires. All he wants to do is be a channel through which a powerful impact can be made on the world. He wants to be like a wire that is filled with electricity from a power source or like a pipe through which water can flow coming from a reservoir. 1 Cor. 3:5 (NLT), "After all, who is Apollos? Who is Paul? We are only God's servants through whom you believed the Good News. Each of us did the work the Lord gave us." Notice the phrase "through whom." Apollos and Paul were vessels through whom God worked. This tells us God uses people who are surrendered to Him.

Paul said, "It is through us that you believed. God gave us a message, and He allowed us to preach it. It was through us that you came to know Him." In Rom. 15:18 Paul said God worked "through me, resulting in the obedience of the Gentiles." God kept using Paul because he remained surrendered to Him at all times. 2 Tim. 4:17, "But the Lord stood with me and strengthened me, so that the message might be preached fully through me." Become the type of vessel through whom God can do His work. You allow God to accomplish what He wants to accomplish through your willful obedience. To be used by God you must grow up and start living in the light of your faith, all the while pledging allegiance to the Lamb and living a surrendered life to the will of God. A servant of God does not say, "God, what can You do for me today?" Rather, they say, "Lord, what can I do for You today?" Consider it a privilege to be allowed to do the things God wants you to do.

It is not a burden to be a love servant; it is a position of great honor. Why? Because it makes you more like Jesus who said, "For even the Son of Man did not come to be served, but to serve, and to give His life as a ransom for many" (Matt. 20:28). The Master is greater than the disciple, yet He washed the feet of the disciples (John 13:3-5). Indeed, Jesus is the ultimate example of a servant in God's kingdom. Jesus set the example for all of us to follow. He came to pour out His life in service to others. He healed the sick, raised the dead, fed the hungry, accepted the outcasts. After washing the disciples' feet, Jesus said, "If I then, your Lord and teacher, have washed your feet, you also ought to wash one another's feet. For I have given you an example, that you should do just as I have done to you. Truly I say to you, a servant is not greater than his master" (John 13:14-16). In God's kingdom, greatness is measured by the extent we are willing to serve one another humbly. Jesus showed us what to do. May we follow His example always.

1 Cor. 3:9 says we are "fellow workers" with God. This describes a divine partnership where you are God are intimately entwined together. The work is His and you are the vessel through which the work gets done. He uses servants who are surrendered and who cooperate with Him. Partners always work together. You provide the body through which God can work, and He provides the grace and enabling power to get the work done. When God calls you to do His work, it is not be-

cause He needs your strength - it is because He desires your surrender. The work has always been His. The power has always been His. The plan, the wisdom, the results - these are all His from beginning to end. You are the vessel through which His purposes flow. A vessel does not boast in the water it carries; it only yields to the One who fills it. In the same way, God pours His grace, His compassion, His power, and His Kingdom purposes into those who are willing to be used.

God does not look for the strongest, the most talented, or the most qualified. He looks for the surrendered. He looks for hearts that say, "Lord, I am yours. Work through me." When you cooperate with Him - when you align your will with His - He accomplishes through you what you could never accomplish on your own. Your part is obedience. His part is everything else. Rest in the truth knowing you are not carrying the mission; the mission carries you. You are not the source; you are the instrument. As long as you stay surrendered, God will continue to use you, shape you, and flow through you for His glory. Say to Him, "Lord, do Your work in me, and do Your work through me." In 1 Cor. 3:10, Paul said the work he did for God was "according to the grace of God which was given to me." God was by Paul's side helping him every step of the way. Impacting the world is always enabled by the grace of God. You don't make the world a better place with your own ability, you do it according to God's unfailing grace.

Paul said this grace was given to him. It was a gift from God. It was God in him and working through him that affected what Paul was able to do. The good news is God has given you this same grace. 1 Cor. 1:4 says, "I thank my God always concerning you for the grace of God which was given to you by Christ Jesus." God gave this grace to all believers. We all have access to the enabling power of God. This is why we never have an excuse. His works are now enabled in our life. If you are saved, you have access to the enabling power of God's grace. 2 Tim. 2:1 says, "You, therefore, my son, be strong in the grace that is in Christ Jesus." It is an incredible thing to be partners with God. If He lives in you and you partake of Him, He'll enable you to do what He commands you to do. It is God's clear intention that every one of His people be used to impact the world. Until the Lord returns, that is the only calling there is.

Most people are not serving God on a daily basis. But if you truly know God, you'll never be happy sitting on the bench doing nothing. No, you want to be in the game. This is why you say every day, "Here I am! Use me today!" Your life is not complete unless each day you make a positive difference in someone's life. After all, that's what you're here for, that's the reason you were created. You're here to help make the world a better place, to help make the lives of other people better. The Bible calls people like this "vessels for honor" (1 Tim. 2:21), people whose lives are intended for honorable purposes, a person "prepared for every good work." NLT, "If you keep yourself pure, you will be a utensil God can use for His purpose. Your life will be clean, and you will be ready for the Master to use for every good work." God only uses clean vessels, people free from willful and habitual sin. You need to take stern action against evil and remove every sinful influence in your life.

To be a vessel of honor you've got to remove everything from your old life that would taint and stain your new life in Christ. W. E. Vine said, "We are to keep ourselves pure in both doctrine and practice, and to avoid identifying ourselves with those who do not walk in moral uprightness." 2 Cor. 5:17 says, "Therefore, if anyone is in Christ, he is a new creation; old things have passed away, behold, all things have become new." Live a clean life and you'll be a vessel for honor that God can use. God said Paul was "a chosen vessel of Mine to bear My name before Gentiles" (Acts 9:15). A vessel is used to contain things. For God to use us as vessels, we must be empty, clean, and available. He will then fill us with grace and power to be used for His glory. Kenneth Wuest says the cleansed man "shall be as instruments highly prized." He'll be sanctified, set apart for God's possession and use. 2 Tim. 2:21 says a sanctified vessel is "useful to the Master."

The Greek word "euchrestos" pertains to being helpful, beneficial, and very profitable. This Greek word conveys the sense of that which is easy to make use of. Does this describe you? Do you make yourself available and easy for God to use? Paul said Mark was "useful to me for ministry" (2 Tim. 4:11). A useful vessel is valuable, helpful, and furnishes what is needed at the time. A clean, holy vessel is prepared for every good work. They are forever ready for God to pour His grace and power through them. Titus 3:1 says we should all "be prepared and ready to do any upright and honorable work." The Message Bible says you are to be "always ready to lend a helping hand." Always be in a state of readiness to be used for the Master's work. Vessels for honor should be on the tiptoes of expectancy every hour of every day. When the call to impact the world comes your way, you must be ready and primed to respond without delay or hesitation.

Remember, God only uses clean vessels. Christian author Chester A. Pennington said, "No amount of good deeds can make us good persons. We must be good before we can do good." Repent of your sins so you'll be ready to recognize the opportunities God graciously gives. Martin Luther said, "Oh, it is a living, busy, active, mighty thing, this faith. And so it is impossible for it not to do good works incessantly. It does not ask whether there are good works to do, but before the question arises it has already done them and is always at the doing of them. He who does not these works is a faithless man. He knows neither what faith is or what good works are, though he talks and talks with many words about faith and good works." Count it a privilege to influence the lives of other people. Oswald Chambers said, "Do good until it is an unconscious habit of life and you do not know you are doing it." Every morning brings with it a new day of opportunities to make this world a better place. Don't let these opportunities pass you by.

| 11 |

"APPLE OF HIS EYE"

Eph. 4:1 says, "Therefore I, a prisoner for serving the Lord, beg you to lead a life worthy of your calling, for you have been called by God." When God places His hand upon your life, He doesn't call you according to your abilities, He calls you according to His purpose. You were chosen with intention, separated with love, and appointed with destiny. Heaven has spoken your name, and because of that, your life carries weight, meaning, and divine responsibility. The Amplified Bible says, "I beg you to walk and lead a life worthy of the divine calling to which you have been called with behavior that is a credit to the summons to God's service." Make no mistake about it, you have been called by God to impact the world. You've been summoned by God to influence others and to make this world a better place. The Message Bible says, "I want you to get out there and walk - better yet, run! - on the road God called you to travel. I don't want anyone strolling down some path that goes nowhere." Let it not escape your thinking that the call on your life preceded the creation of the world.

You are not an accident. You were born on purpose with an assignment from on high to fulfill. You carry a calling that predates creation itself. Your calling is older than the world and nothing in the world can cancel it. And if God began it in eternity, nothing in time can stop it. Not your past, not your fears, not your mistakes, not the opinions of others. What God spoke over your life before the world began still stands today. So walk boldly and stand confidently. Live with the assurance that you were chosen on purpose, for a purpose, before time began. God has gone before you, and what He planned for you will come to pass. He wants you to live a life worthy of your calling and this is why Heb. 12:1 (AMP) says, "Let us run with patient endurance and steady and active persistence the appointed course of the race that is set before us." In other words, keep on keeping on. Keep running until you've impacted the world in a positive, powerful way. Run the race until the world becomes a better place.

How do you run a race? First, you get a trainer. Rely on the Holy Spirit for His help. Next, you follow a game plan. Read God's Word. Finally, you work out regularly. Put your faith into action. Run the race set before you. Don't stroll, don't wander around aimlessly. The Greek word for "run" is "trecho" and it refers to 'moving forward rapidly.' Time is short so live your call. Advance speedily and move forward with full effort and purpose. 1 Cor. 9:24 says, "Run in such a way that you may win." Paul is describing a runner who is intent on getting to the finish line as quickly as possible. He's saying don't jog, don't walk slowly, don't sit down and don't lay down. Run your race with concentration of purpose and singleness of aim. Be consumed with a holy love for God and with a passion for the well-being of others. Much is at stake and many people are counting on you. This is why you must be prepared to endure with patience, courage, and cheerfulness.

Keep your eyes focused on the prize that awaits you. Focus on what is beyond the current pressures you're going through. Focus on a better world in which we can all live. You can run your race with confidence knowing God is in control. Eph. 1:11 says, "He chose us in advance, and He makes everything work out according to His plan." You don't have to run through life wondering if everything will fall apart. You don't have to approach your future with fear in your eyes or trembling in your steps. You can run your race with boldness, with assurance, and with holy confidence because God is in control. When you understand that God has already prepared the path before you, you stop running like someone who's uncertain. You start running like someone who's chosen, like someone who's covered, like someone who's carried by the grace of God. The pressure to figure everything out lifts, because you realize the outcome is in His hands, not yours.

Lift your head, strengthen your stride, and keep moving forward. God is not only with you but He is guiding you, shaping you, and working all things for your good and His glory. Run your race with confidence and never make light of the magnitude of your call. So huge is the call of God on your life that Paul prays you'll get a true revelation of how big it is. He prayed in Eph. 1:18,19 that you would "grasp the immensity of this glorious way of life He has for His followers, oh, the utter extravagance of His work in us who trust Him - endless energy, boundless strength! I also pray that you will understand the incredible greatness of God's power for us who believe Him." How great is this power? Vs. 20 says it's the same power the Father used when he raised Christ from the dead and seated Him at His right hand in the heavenly places." When you run your race there is great power pushing you forward. Victory is assured because no weapon formed against you will prosper (Is. 54:17).

As Jesus sits in victory and power and authority at the right hand of the Father, you are sitting there with Him. That is your position as a child of God. You don't set out to change the world in fear and trembling. Eph. 1:23 (NLT) says you are "made full and complete by Christ, who fills all things everywhere with Himself." Wherever you go, Christ with all His power goes with you. Don't be afraid of the devil, make him be afraid of you. Make him tremble every morning when you wake up. Determine every day to wake up with purpose, wake up with praise, wake up knowing that you carry the light of Christ, and darkness cannot stand in the presence of light. The devil's greatest weapon is intimidation, but he loses his power the moment you realize who you are: a blood-bought, Spirit-filled, God-anointed warrior. You are a co-laborer with Christ and there is no way you can fail. You can run your race and change the world knowing God "always causes us to triumph in Christ" (2 Cor. 2:14).

The last thing you want to do is let the devil convince you that you're unworthy to be used by God. Low self-esteem and not knowing who you are in Christ will prevent your call from being fulfilled. Paul addresses this is Eph. 2:10 where he says, "For we are God's workmanship created in Christ Jesus to do good works, which God prepared in advance for us to do." The Greek word for "workmanship" is "poiema" and it's where we get the word "poem" from. Paul is saying you are God's poem, a person of grace and beauty. The NLT says you are "God's masterpiece" and the AMP says you are "God's own handiwork" and the NJB says you are "God's work of art." The word "workmanship" refers to more than the product of creation, it also refers to the degree of skill with which the product is made. Ps. 139:14 says, "I will praise You, for I am fearfully and wonderfully made; Marvelous are Your works, and that my soul knows very well." This speaks of the care and attention with which God made us.

The Message Bible says, "I was sculpted from nothing into something." That degree of skill imparts value to the thing made. The value of a thing is derived from the talents of the person who designed and created it. We are God's workmanship because He created us. He formed us into the person He wanted us to be for His own good pleasure and for His purposes. Everything God creates is of high value. God's greatest masterpiece of all creation is each of us. He made you and you belong to Him to do as He chooses. God put forth His most powerful and creative effort to make you who you are. He's like a poet who has the extraordinary ability to write a literary masterpiece. Rick Renner said, "There's nothing cheap about you at all! God's creative, artistic, intelligent genius went into your making. Look how much you've been given in Jesus

Christ!" God took you into His hands and released His most creative forces and made you a person who would be worthy to bear His name.

God turned you into something spectacular. You are made in His image and have great worth and value in His eyes. Indeed, you are "the apple of His eye" (Ps. 17:8). Ponder for a moment the wonderful truth that your life is the Father's poem, authored by the Lamb, and enabled by the power of the Holy Spirit. Think of your life as the canvas on which the Master is producing a work of art which will bring Him eternal praise and glory. Now and forevermore, you are God's eternal possession. Titus 2:14 (NLT) says Jesus came "to make us His very own people, totally committed to doing good deeds." The Message Bible says Jesus made "us a people He can be proud of, energetic in goodness." This goes along with Eph. 2:10 that says you were created "for good works." That's why you're here, to live out and fulfill your heavenly call. You were created to do good works, to impact the lives of others, to make the world a better place, to influence those around you.

Over and over again scripture tells us that the very purpose of our existence on planet earth is to do good works each and every day. Col. 1:10 says you are to "walk in a manner worthy of the Lord, to please Him in all respects, bearing fruit in every good work." The Message Bible says, "We pray that you'll live well for the Master, making Him proud of you as you work hard in His orchard." Jesus said in Matt. 5:16, "Let your light shine before men in such a way that they may see your good works, and glorify your Father who is in heaven." 2 Cor. 9:8

says we are to "abound to every good work" and Heb. 13:16 says, "Do not forget to do good and to share, for with such sacrifices God is well pleased." Gal. 6:10 says, "Therefore, as we have opportunity, let us do good to all, especially to those who are of the household of faith." MSG, "Every time we get the chance, let us work for the benefit of all, starting with the people closest to us in the community of faith."

Charles Spurgeon said, "He wishes us not only to produce good works, but to abound in them. He would have us become imitators of Himself as dear children." God has woven purpose into the very fabric of your being. Every single day of your life carries divine potential. Every conversation can be a seed. Every act of kindness can be a light. Every sacrifice can be an offering placed before the Lord. Every morning presents you with another opportunity to fulfill your purpose and to be good to people whose lives intersect with yours. Wake up each day with a genuine, sincere, loving, Spirit-empowered, God-glorifying eagerness to impact the world by your service to others. Be known for your consistent and aggressive goodness done out of an unselfish love for God and other people for this is the purpose for which you have been called. Wake up each morning with purpose because true fulfillment comes from allowing God to use us to make a difference in the lives of others.

Ask the Lord to show you the good works He has prepared for you. Let your life be a vessel through which His love flows, His compassion shines, and His goodness transforms the world around you. For this is why you are here: to do good, to love deeply, and to glorify God with every step we take. God didn't place you here merely to exist but to invest. Every act of kindness, every word of encouragement, every moment you choose to serve rather than be served becomes a deposit of heaven into the life of someone else. Your time, your love, your compassion, your patience, your gifts, and your faithfulness are all treasures God has placed in your hands. The world becomes richer every time you pour them out. Your life is a vessel designed to overflow so keep shining, keep giving, and keep sowing good into the soil of this world. Why? Because your life, lived unto God, is a gift that keeps on giving. Indeed, someone's miracle may be waiting on your willingness to contribute what only you can give.

Your good works are your contribution to the world. You're here to use your life to make a donation into the lives of others. You are God's masterpiece, but it's only revealed when you fulfill your calling. Your true beauty and greatness shine forth when you bear fruit for the kingdom. Never underestimate what God can and will do through your submission to His will and purpose. The sky is the limit on the impact you can make on this world. Never forget that your calling is a divine invitation from God to be a co-laborer with Him, to work alongside Him to make this world a better place. God wants you to "know what is the hope of His calling" (Eph. 1:18). He tells you who you are and what you are to do. He then invites you to live out your meaning and purpose. This calling from God is a high, holy, and heavenly calling. It's bigger than life itself for God has uniquely gifted you to impact this world for His glory. The church isn't a building you go to once a week;

you are the church. You're called out and sent by God into all the world.

There are three things to which God has called you to. First, He calls you to salvation. Before God calls you to fulfill your ministry, He calls you to Himself. 2 Peter 3:9 says God "is extraordinarily patient toward you not wishing that any should perish, but that all should come to repentance." Second, He calls you to sanctification (1 Thess. 4:3). You have been set apart and you are to be different from those in this wicked, ungodly world. You are called to live a holy life. 1 Peter 1:15 says, "As He who called you is holy, you also be holy in all your conduct." Do this and you'll be set apart for special use. Third, God calls you to service. He first calls you to Himself. He then calls you to be transformed. Next, He calls you to engage with others, using you to make an impact on this world. Embrace the call to service that is on your life. God can and will use you in a unique, powerful way. There is nothing more fulfilling than that.

As a follower of Christ you have been chosen by God, set apart, gifted, enabled, and empowered to fulfill a very unique calling. You have been called by God and if you haven't been fulfilling your purpose for being here then right away you need to reclaim your calling. Take time out from your busy schedule to ponder the fact that God wants you to live a life worthy of His calling (Eph. 4:1). Setting out to fulfill your calling will sustain you, it will keep you going. You'll finish your race no matter how hard the devil tries to stop you. Phil. 3:14 (NLT) says, "I press on to reach the end of the race and receive the heavenly prize for which God, through Christ Jesus, is calling us." The

Message Bible says, "I've got my eye on the goal, where God is beckoning us onward. I'm off and running, and I'm not turning back. "When troubles arise don't look at what you're going through but focus on where you're going to. Focus on the prize that awaits you and you'll be sustained all the way.

What an honor it is to know you've been created by God to do something significant, meaningful, and eternal, something that really, really matters, to know that the God who formed the universe also formed you intentionally, purposefully, and lovingly. You were created to do something meaningful, something eternal, something that really, really matters. The world may overlook you, but heaven never does. God entrusts assignments only to those He has prepared, and He has prepared you. You carry divine purpose and when you use your life for what God created you to do, you're not just making a difference - you're fulfilling destiny. Yes, you've been uniquely created by God for His glory. God receives great honor when you influence others and make a positive difference in this world. Determine to live from the inside out because there is something inside of you that craves for spiritual and lasting significance. Somewhere, somehow, you want your life to count for something.

Deep down inside of you is a knowing that your birth was no accident and that you were created for a reason, a calling, a purpose, a divine destiny. Inside of you is a longing for more than financial success or a nice house to live in or a membership at some prestigious country club. There is something inside of you that craves for spiritual and lasting significance.

Somewhere, somehow, you want your life to count for something. Rich people in the world often fall into depression and some even commit suicide because their life has no meaning. All they have is wealth and power and that is not enough to fill the void in their life. Your life will dramatically change for the better when you recognize that you've been genuinely set apart by God, chosen by God, gifted by God, and called by God. Living with divine purpose is what a good life is all about. Life has little or no meaning if you don't know why you're here and what you were created to do. Seek the Lord and you'll soon find that His will for your life is to be a blessing to others.

| 12 |

"REDEEMING THE TIME"

G od is not looking for spectators in His kingdom, He is looking for active participants, people who will pick up the mantel and fulfill the call on their lives. Your call from God is so very important. It's what lifts you up from a lowly place and seats you in the heavenly realm with Christ Jesus. For sure, your call from God is more important than you realize. It is not just an assignment or a task - it is a divine elevation. God's call reaches down into the low places of your life, into the moments when you feel unseen, unworthy, or overlooked, and it lifts you into a realm you could never reach on your own. So great is this call that even the apostle Paul says you will have a hard time comprehending it with the limits of your humanity. Eph. 1:18 says, "I pray that the eyes of your understanding may be enlightened in order that you may know the hope to which you have been called." Go to God and He will reveal to you what your calling is. It's the understanding of your call that leads you to live a purpose driven life.

Once you know what your call is, Paul says in Eph. 4:1, "Therefore I, a prisoner for serving the Lord, beg you to lead a life worthy of your calling, for you have been called by God." Walk in the confidence of someone who has been chosen, raised up, and set apart. Every man and woman in the kingdom of God should be a person of action. God wants you to get up off the chair of comfort and go out into the world and do something good and positive. The essence of your call is always action. People of action take the love of God into all situations of need, into all the places where people are victims of hard times. They reach out to others to answer their call for help in times of crisis, disaster, and great need. They help meet calls for physical, spiritual, and financial support. Being a person of action can be challenging but with God all things are possible. Missionary C. T. Studd said, "God is not looking for nibblers of the possible, but for grabbers of the impossible."

Rom. 13:11 (AMP) says, "It is high time now for you to wake up out of your sleep." The Message Bible says don't "doze off, oblivious to God." God is sounding an alarm in this hour. Not a soft whisper, not a gentle nudge - an alarm. Why? Because too many hearts have drifted into spiritual drowsiness. It's not that people have rejected God; it's that they've become oblivious to Him. They've been distracted by routine, numbed by comfort, stifled by busyness. And slowly, silently, the fire begins to fade. But God's Word calls us back to alertness. "Wake up." Not tomorrow. Not when life gets easier. Not when you feel more ready. Now. To wake up spiritually means to sharpen your awareness of God's presence, to recognize the urgency of His call, and to live with purpose rather than passivity. It means refusing to sleepwalk through your destiny. It means noticing the opportunities God is placing in front of you, the people He wants you to reach, the changes He is urging you to make.

You need to wake up because you can't fight spiritual battles while asleep. You can't walk in your calling while dreaming and you can't shine your light while your eyes are closed. God is moving right now and He wants you wide awake, fully alert, and actively engaged. This is a moment of spiritual awakening, a time to rise up in faith, shake off complacency, and say, "Lord, I'm ready. Speak, and I will respond." Don't doze off. Don't drift. Don't settle. Wake up because God is ready to use you today. Rom. 13:14 (MSG) says, "Get out of bed and get dressed! Don't loiter and linger, waiting until the very last minute. Dress yourselves in Christ and be up and about." Paul is clearly seeking to convey to his readers a strong sense of urgency. He is saying that time is running out and opportunities are fleeting. The time to take action is now! There is no time for apathy, complacency, or indifference. Life is short and before you know it darkness will come when no one can work (John 9:4).

Men and women of God wake up in the morning and get dressed for action. They take off their night clothes and put on clothes appropriate for the work God called them to do. Living wholeheartedly for God and loving people should be your primary objective in life in view of the brief time we have left on the earth. An anonymous writer once said, "Life is too short for us to do everything we want to do, but it is long enough for us to do everything God wants us to do." An old familiar saying states that there are three things that never come back - the spent arrow, the spoken word, and the lost opportunity. Poet John Greenleaf Whittier said in the 19th century, "Of all sad words of tongue or pen, the saddest are these: 'It might have been.'" Preacher Thomas Brooks said in the 17th century, "Time is not yours to dispose of as you please. It is a glorious talent that men must be accountable for as well as any other talent."

Eph. 5:14 says, "Awake, you who sleep" and vs. 16 says we are to be "redeeming the time, because the days are evil." The Message Bible says, "Use your head. Make the most of every chance you get. These are desperate times. Don't live carelessly, unthinkingly. Make sure you understand what the Master wants" (vs. 16,17). There is always enough time to do God's will. Instead of counting the days wondering how much time is left or how quickly life is moving, choose to make your days count. Every sunrise is a new invitation to walk in purpose. Every moment is a chance to love, to serve, to grow, to obey, and to reflect Christ. To spend your time wisely, you must spend it in eternity. Know with certainty that God will never call you to a task without providing the time, strength, and grace to fulfill it. Heaven's assignments are never rushed; they are perfectly timed. What God purposes, He also empowers.

Do not waste what little time you've been given. Will Rogers once said, "Half our life is spent trying to find something to do with the time we have rushed through life to save." Most time is wasted not in hours but in minutes. A bucket with a small hole in the bottom gets just as empty as a bucket that is deliberately kicked over. Opportunities do not wait. You must seize them before they pass you by. John MacArthur said, "Wisdom numbers the days, sees the limited time, and buys the opportunity. Don't be foolish, shun opportunities for evil but seize opportunities for good." Gal. 6:10, "Therefore, as we have opportunity, let us do good to all, especially to those who are of the household of faith." This verse is saying we might not always have the opportunity to do good. God sets boundaries around our lives and our opportunity for service exists only within those boundaries. Make the most of your time on earth fulfilling God's purposes. The brevity of life is a strong argument for making the best use of every opportunity God gives us.

Put yourself in a position to always be led by the Spirit and He'll enable you to be on high alert for spiritual opportunities you can seize before they are gone. Walk wisely. Be led by the Spirit. Redeem the time. Don't be like Mark Twain who said, "I was seldom able to see an opportunity until it had ceased to be one." Alexander Graham Bell said, "When one door closes, another one opens, but we often look so long and so regretfully upon the closed door that we do not see the one that has been opened for us." God gives every person opportunities to impact the world. Doors for service are opened each and every day and with it comes vast potential to make this world a better place. Every single day, God places before us fresh opportunities - quiet invitations to touch a life, heal a wound, lift a burden, or shine His light into someone's darkness. These opportunities may come disguised as simple moments: a conversation, a need, a burden on our heart, or a chance to serve when no one else is looking.

God is always opening doors. You can achieve your full potential in your service to the Lord only as you utilize and make the most of the opportunities He gives you. Some are small and subtle; others swing wide with unmistakable purpose. But each carries the potential to change the world in ways you may never fully see. When you step through these doors with faith, humility, and courage, we participate in God's ongoing work of restoration and love. You were created with purpose. You were placed here with intention. And every day, heaven aligns moments for you to make this world a better place. Don't underestimate the power of a kind word, a helping hand, or a simple act of obedience. These are the seeds God uses to grow miracles. Walk boldly. Serve willingly. And trust that with every open door, God is giving you the chance to leave His mark on the world through your life. Billy graham once said, "Life is a glorious opportunity if it is used to condition us for eternity. If we fail in this, though we succeed in everything else, our life will have been a failure."

Charles Swindoll said, "We are all faced with a series of great opportunities brilliantly disguised as impossible situations." Just remember, with God all things are possible. English writer John Ruskin said, "Sojourn in every place as if you meant to spend your life there, never omitting an opportunity of doing a kindness, speaking a true word, or making a friend." There is great and eternal value in all the good things you do with your life; in the continuous activity you put forth to influence the lives of other people. Every act of kindness, every word of encouragement, every moment you choose to love instead of turning away are seeds sown into eternity. Heaven never overlooks what you do with a sincere heart. Even the actions that seem small in your eyes are woven into God's greater story of redemption. He is glorified and the lives of other people are made better. The work you do is energized by the power of God and is work that lasts for all eternity.

Your continuous activity to influence the lives of others is not wasted. Each day when you rise up and choose compassion, speak truth, or lend strength to someone who is struggling, you are partnering with God's purposes. You are shaping destinies, lifting burdens, and revealing the heart of Christ through your life. Sometimes you may not see the results. Sometimes your efforts feel unnoticed or unappreciated. But in the Kingdom of God, nothing done in love disappears. God records every sacrifice, every prayer, every act of service. What you do for others echoes far beyond this life - impacting generations, healing hearts, and building an eternal legacy. You are a vessel of divine purpose, and every good thing you do carries eternal weight. God sees it and heaven honors it when someone's life is better today because you chose to use yours for good. Time is of the essence. Kent Hughes said, "Each ache, pain, gray hair, new wrinkle, or funeral is another reminder that it is later that it has even been before."

Yes, time is quickly passing by. It's later than you think and you must redeem the time you have left. Now is the time to "love your neighbor as yourself" (Mark 12:31). Who is your neighbor? It's any person God has put in your way whom you can bless. May God help all of us love others with a sense of urgency and selflessness. Be intentional as you watch for and seize opportunities to do good. Ask God to give you eyes to see those whom you are to bless, those whose lives you can make better. Follow the exhortation of John Wesley who said, "Do all the good you can, in all the ways you can, to all the people you can, as long as ever you can." Bible teacher Richard De-Haan said, "The giver of time is God Himself, and that places a far greater value upon it than any monetary figure could suggest. We must therefore use our time intelligently taking advantage of the opportunities it provides us to serve the Lord and to do His will."

The clock is ticking and every moment counts. All men and women who have gone to sleep spiritually need to wake up and love their neighbor while they have the opportunity to do so. The Encyclopedia Britannica defines the word "sleep" as 'a state of inactivity with a loss of consciousness and a decrease in responsiveness to events taking place.' Paul is telling all those who are spiritually asleep to wake up and do something good with their life. He wants them to hear the call of God while there is still time to do so. To awake from slumber, you must reconnect with your God-given purpose. There is a reason you're alive and you can't fall asleep on that vital truth. You must have a burning passion to be activated into God's service, into doing the things God created for you to do long before you were even born (Eph. 2:10). When you embrace the call of God on your life you'll wake up from the sluggish, hypnotic, trance-like state the world tries to pull you into.

Stop going through the motions and start living with a new sense of urgency. Wake up and tap into the great potential that resides on the inside of you. Living for Jesus is not a part-time job. With great enthusiasm for righteous living and serving God you'll accomplish much as you set out to change the world. You must live your call each and every day and it all starts with making yourself available for the Master's use. It's when you say, "Here I am! Send me" (Is. 6:8). Give your life to Jesus and surrender your will to His will. Be aggressive in what you do. Actively look for needs in people's live and go help meet that need. Rom. 12:11 (NLT) says, "Never be lazy, but work hard and serve the Lord enthusiastically." The Message Bible says, "Don't burn out; keep yourselves fueled and aflame." The Phillips Bible says, "Let us not allow slackness to spoil our work and let us keep the fires of the spirit burning, as we do our work for God."

A person who is "fervent in spirit" (NKJB) is so enthusiastic about their work for God that they can hardly contain their excitement. The key to impacting the world is to always make yourself available to God to be used for His divine purposes, anytime, anywhere. The power of availability is strong. It's what shatters the evil intentions of the enemy. It's what opens every door that needs to be opened. No matter how big or small the task, always make yourself available to God. Have a willingness to go anywhere and do anything. Availability is being willing to adjust your schedule, your agenda, and your plans to fit the desires of God and other people. It makes personal priorities secondary to the needs of those around you. God will use you to embrace people and lift them up when you make yourself available to Him. Put availability into action. If you'll do that, the power of God that is flowing through the universe will be available for you to use.

Consider the vastness of the potential you have when this power is working in you and through you. Lives will be changed, and this world will become a better place. Your availability to God is based on the love you have for Him. God wants you to be wholly devoted to Him so that your love for Him will flow out to others. Your time, talents, and treasures should flow willfully out of you with joy and gladness. Cheerfully you want to bless others even if you have to pay a price to do so. Always share what you have with others. Heb. 13:6 says, "But do not forget to do good and to share, for with such sacrifices God is well pleased." Present yourself for service and God will definitely use you to be kind and good to others, to be generous and contribute to the needy. Charles Spurgeon said, "I long to see Christian friends everywhere who will not wait to be asked but will make the Lord's business their business. Let your gift be an outburst of a free and gracious spirit which takes a delight in showing that it does not praise God in word only, but indeed and in truth."

At age twelve Jesus was found "in the temple, sitting in the midst of the teachers, both listening to them and asking them questions" (Luke 2:46). When told that his family had been looking for Him, He responded, "Why is it that you sought Me? Did you not know that I must be about My Father's business?" (vs. 49). In other words, Jesus was asking, "Why didn't you know where to look? There is only one place I could possibly be." Let the same thing be said of you. If people are looking for you, let them always find you out and about doing the Father's business. Like Jesus, have a consciousness of the work God has called you to do. Make it clear to all that the top priority of your life is to make a positive impact in the world. Even at age twelve Jesus was moved by a divine compulsion to do the Father's will. He knew it was a necessity that He be about the Father's business. He said He must do this. He then said in Luke 4:43, "I must preach the kingdom of God to other cities also, for I was sent for this purpose.

Jesus was a man on a mission. He had a purpose which He intentionally fulfilled. Since you are made in His image, the same thing needs to be said of you. Like Jesus, you are to be obedient to the Father's will and be about the Father's business. You are to endure opposition and never lose heart (Heb. 12:3). You are a person on a mission for God, a person of love and sacrifice. You have the determination to fulfill God's will no matter what the cost may be (Is. 50:7). You are forever ready to put God first, not just in theory but in action. You'll be an instrument of power when you make yourself available to Him. Availability is a state of listening and responding. You look for needs and then take the initiative to meet them. You go the extra mile and do what nobody else wants to do. Availability means there are no strings attached in what you're willing to do. It's present in the midst of any unconditional act of live. Availability is how you imitate the love that God has for each of us. The good news is your availability in little things leads to availability in great things.

| 13 |

"A FOUNTAIN OF LIFE"

Don't let the thought of impacting the world overwhelm you. Don't let the vastness of this planet cause you to think you have nothing to give. Sometimes a simple word of encouragement is all a person needs to set their life straight. God has designed your words to carry tremendous power to heal, to strengthen, and to redirect a weary heart. Prov. 15:23 says, "A word spoken in due season, how good it is!" There are moments when someone is standing on the edge of giving up, silently praying for a sign, a reminder, or even just a whisper of hope. In those moments, God may choose you to be His voice. One sincere word can break the weight of discouragement and lift a soul back into the light. Encouragement doesn't have to be long or eloquent. It just needs to be timely, sincere, and full of grace. When you slow down, listen to the Holy Spirit, and speak life into others, you become an instrument of God's love planting seeds that may transform someone's entire direction.

Yes, speaking the right words at the right time can make all the difference in the world. They can refresh, strengthen, build up, inspire, and gladden the hearts of those you speak to. Prov. 25:11 says a word spoken at the proper time "is like apples of gold in settings of silver." This shows how valuable your words can be. It is not only what you say but how and when you say it. Sometimes the right word at just the right time can change the whole course of a person's life. Is. 50:4 says, "The Lord God has given me His words of wisdom that I should know how to speak a word in season to him who is weary." The Message Bible says, "The Master, God, has given me a well-taught tongue, so I know how to encourage tired people." Let your words be gentle. Let them be intentional. Let them be guided by God. You never know whose life will be set back on course because you were willing to speak a "due season" word. Someone's breakthrough may be waiting on your voice.

Timely words are delightful, good, pleasant, and agreeable. They're so well composed that they bring great benefit to those who hear them. Eph. 4:29 says, "Let everything you say be good and helpful so that your words will be an encouragement to those who hear them." Do not say something when it is not the right moment to do so. Think before you speak. Trust the Holy Spirit to guide the timing of your words. When you do speak, Col. 4:6 says, "Let your speech always be with grace, seasoned with salt, that you may know how you ought to answer each one." The NLT says, "Let your conversation be gracious and effective" and the Message Bible says, "The goal is to bring out the best in others in a conversation." God has given you the ability to speak life, healing, hope, and wisdom into the hearts of those around you. When Scripture tells you to let our speech be filled with grace, it is calling you to speak from a place of love, patience, and divine influence.

Grace means giving people more kindness than they expect and more mercy than they deserve, just as God has done for you. And your words must also be seasoned with salt. Salt preserves, purifies, and gives flavor. In the same way, your words should preserve peace, purify discouragement, and add flavor to someone's day. Salted speech isn't harsh, it's purposeful. It brings clarity, truth, and God's perspective in a way that strengthens rather than tears down. When grace and salt come together, you begin to speak with heavenly wisdom. You know how to answer each person not out of impulse, but out of spiritual maturity. You respond instead of reacting, you bless instead of criticizing, you uplift instead of burden. Today, ask the Holy Spirit to sit on your tongue. Let Him guide your conversations, your responses, and even your silence. May your words reflect the nature of Christ so that everyone who hears you encounters His love.

You'll be able to influence people in a positive way with words that are charming in an open and delightful way, words spoken with sincerity and truth. Your words should be "winsome" which Webster's Dictionary says is 'attractive, appealing, generally pleasing and engaging often because of a childlike charm and innocence.' The Greek Expository says, "By the sweetness and courtesy of their conversation they are to impress favorably the heathen." In other words, be graciously spiritual in all you say and do. You are a citizen of heaven, and your words and actions should have a heavenly scent to them. The words of a wise man are like silver (Prov. 10:20), a tree of life (Prov. 15:4), food (Prov. 10:21), refreshing water (Prov. 10:11), and medicine (Prov. 12:18). The words of Jesus captivated those who listened to Him (Luke 4:22). Likewise, your words should always be pleasant, attractive, a sign of divine favor.

Paul says you're to put salt into your speech and keep your words pure and honest, to always speak in a manner that will be pleasing to God. Natural salt purifies, cleanses, preserves from corruption. When seasoned with salt, words of beauty and eloquence become vessels of grace. You should speak in such a way that your words will build up a person and not tear them down. Just as salt brings out flavor, preserves what is precious, and heals what is wounded, your words carry the power to restore life to those who are weary. When seasoned with salt, words of beauty and eloquence will cheer up and enrich those desperately longing for a word of encouragement. When your speech is seasoned by the Spirit, it becomes more than conversation; it becomes ministry. There are people all around you who are quietly hurting, silently hoping, and desperately longing for just one word that reminds them they are seen, valued, and loved by God.

A simple phrase can lift a bowed head. A gentle encouragement can steady a trembling heart. A sincere compliment can awaken courage. A timely scripture can anchor the soul. And a compassionate response can turn someone's entire day toward hope. Speak with the beauty and eloquence that flows from a heart aligned with Christ. The Bible teaches us that salt enhances flavor (Job 6:6), symbolizes keeping a promise (Mark 18:19), speaks of goodness (Mark 9:50), and indicates purity in speech (Col. 4:6). Always let your words be seasoned with salt. Be the type of person who enhances the lives of those around you, a person characterized by integrity and goodness. Be led by the Spirit and the love of God in you will become evident not only in what you say but also in how and when you say it. Ask God to help you use wholesome words that bring honor to Him. Prov. 21:23, "Whoever guards his mouth and tongue keeps his soul from troubles."

A real man and woman of God is to always speak heaven's language. Oftentimes all it takes is one well-timed sentence to turn a person's midnight hour into morning's light. Be careful to speak in a manner that glorifies God. So great is the power of words that they can make the difference between life and death. Your words should always be gracious. Strive to say all the good that can be said. Mark Twain said he could live for a whole month on one good compliment. A word spoken in due season helps a person want to live a better life even when times are rough and not going the way they'd like. Know with certainty that opportunities to impact the world are endless. Look for those openings and be forever ready to show sincere kindness and genuine concern for others. Forever know that your words can encourage those who are burdened. Prov. 16:24 says, "Pleasant words are a honeycomb, sweet to the soul and healing to the bones."

Seek God and He'll give you spiritual radar so you can access a situation and make the right reply. You'll say the right words at the right time. "Wise people store up knowledge" (Prov. 10:14) and are "filled richly" with the Word of God (Col. 3:16). Yes, "the mouth of the righteous is a fountain of life" (Prov. 10:11). People who speak wisely are people who store God's truth in their hearts. Prov. 10:13 says, "Wisdom is found on the lips of him who has understanding." Those who are mature and truly walk with God, men and women who know His Word and are led by the Spirit, are able to help others and influence them with godly counsel. A positive impact is made when a righteous man or woman gives the right answer at the right time. This is how the world becomes a better place. Sensing when people are ready and seizing the moment is a hallmark of wisdom. Prov. 15:23 (CEV) says, "Giving the right answer at the right time makes everyone happy." The NASB says, "How delightful is a timely word!"

There will be joy unspeakable when your words cause somebody to be edified in righteousness. A crown of rejoicing will be worn by all. As the showers of rain in their proper season fertilize the ground, words spoken in due season will revive the discouraged and downtrodden soul of others. There is a holy joy that flows from heaven when your words lift someone closer to righteousness. Every time you speak life, every time you strengthen a weary soul or point someone toward the path of truth, something eternal takes place. You are not just sharing encouragement - you are sowing seeds that God Himself will water. When your words edify, when they build up rather than tear down, you become a vessel of divine influence. And scripture teaches that such moments do not go unnoticed by the Lord. There will be joy unspeakable when you stand before Him and see the lives your words touched, the hearts strengthened, and the faith renewed because you dared to speak with grace and truth.

As a child of God you are called not to be passive but to always be an active participant in the lives of others. Thankfully, Paul tells us how to do that in 1 Thess. 5:11, "Therefore encourage, admonish, and exhort one another and edify, strengthen, and build up one another, just as you are doing." The word "encourage" is the Greek word "parakaleo" and it means literally 'to call one alongside; to call one to oneself; to call for; to summon.' Encouragement is not simply saying kind words; it is the ministry of lifting a brother or sister's eyes back to God. It is reminding the weary that God is still faithful, the discouraged that God is still present, and the broken that God still heals. The word is used in the New Testament to urge someone to take action, especially some moral and ethical course of action. You call people to stand beside you so you can give them a word of encouragement to help enable them to handle some difficult situation with confidence and courage. Your words may be the very breath of hope someone needs to keep believing.

Admonishment is love wrapped in truth. It is the courage to speak what is right - even when it is difficult - so that another believer is kept from stumbling or drifting. When done with humility and gentleness, admonishment rescues, protects, and restores. It is a gift, not a rebuke. To exhort is to stir up faith, to call others higher, to challenge them to walk worthy of the calling they have received. Exhortation pushes us beyond complacency and reminds us that we are citizens of a heavenly kingdom, empowered by the Spirit to live boldly for Christ. The Greek word for "edify" is "orkodomeo" and it means 'to build; construct; or erect a dwelling.' As a child of God, you are called to help build people up so they can improve spiritually. The church is strongest when every believer becomes a builder. We build by praying for one another, bearing one another's burdens, speaking scripture to one another, and standing firm together against the enemy's lies.

Your presence, your prayers, and your faithfulness become pillars that hold up others who are struggling. The word "edify" refers to the promotion of spiritual growth and the development of godly character by teaching and by example. Such progress is the result of patient labor. Edification is more than just encouragement. It includes any activity that results in people growing up spiritually and becoming more like Christ. As children of God, we are all commanded to continually carry out the tasks of encouraging and edifying other people. Both are needed in a world of spiritual darkness. Charles Spurgeon said, "The more of this the better. Christian people should constantly converse with one another for mutual edification." And then Scripture adds these powerful words: "just as you are doing." This is not a new assignment but a reminder to keep going. You are already walking in love, already serving, already lifting others. God sees it. Heaven honors it. And the body of Christ is blessed because of it. Continue to speak life, to shine light, to build faith, to love deeply.

The need for encouragement and edification in the world is great, and it is the duty of every true believer to help give people what they need. Always help each other with encouraging words. Paul said in Rom. 14:19 (NLT), "So then, let us aim for harmony in the church and try to build each other up." The Message Bible says in 1 Cor. 14:12, "Since you're so eager to participate in what God is doing, why don't you concentrate on doing what helps everyone in the church?" Paul is saying we're to be zealous for the edification of those we come in contact with. We're to abound and excel in our quest to make the lives of other people better. Let your care for others be marked by active interest and intense enthusiasm. Be full of energy in your effort to impact the world you live in. Heb. 10:24 says, "And let us consider one another in order to stir up love and good works." MSG, "Let's see how inventive we can be in encouraging love and helping out."

Encouragement is oxygen to the soul, and we must take careful note of each other's spiritual welfare. When people need encouragement, God will use you to give it to them. Consider your neighbor's needs and circumstances and then immerse yourself in the meeting of those needs. Flowing out of your inner man will be love and good works. This is the "agape" love of God. It is love that is always unconditional and sacrificial. It is unrestricted and unrestrained. It is the highest form of love there is. It is love that serves with humility and is the virtue that surpasses all others. Agape love can exhibit emotion but is must always exhibit action. Love is the passion of self-giving, and it grows when demands are made on it, by all the opportunities of manifestation. F. B. Meyer said, "Wherever there is true love, there must be giving, and giving to the point of sacrifice. The love that gives counts no cost too great."

Good deeds and kind words flow out of men and women who are ready to serve, those who are vessels of honor who are "prepared for every good work" (2 Tim. 2:21). The Greek word for "prepared" is "hetoimazo" and it means 'to make ready, specifically to make ready beforehand for some purpose, use, or activity.' A clean, holy vessel is always in a state of readiness for God to work in and through them. They adapt themselves to serve by any means possible. They have a heart that is prepared to hear from God at any moment. They make plans accordingly and get ready in advance to receive their marching orders from the Lord. Being ready, willing, and able shows how useful you can be for the Master's work. Very rarely, if ever, does God use people who are not ready to serve. Isaiah was ready when he said to God, "Here I am! Send me" (Is. 6:8). Likewise, you must all make yourself ready at all times to be used by God.

Inherent in this readiness is the idea of willingness and eagerness. No matter how hostile the world around us may be, we must have a genuine, sincere, loving, God-glorifying eagerness to be good to people at all times. Titus 3:14 says, "Our people must learn to devote themselves to doing what is good, in order to provide for urgent needs and not live unproductive lives." Notice that Paul says you must "learn" to maintain good works. This instruction is mandatory because at first doing good doesn't always come naturally. We must be trained to perform works of mercy and charity. The Greek word for "learn" is "manthano" and refers to intentional learning by inquiry and observation. God calls for your devotion, and you must actively learn to do good works. The ability to bless others is infused in us when we got born again so the potential is there. However, the actual doing of good works is a learned skill, much like reading or riding a bike. Part of the Great Commission is teaching people to do good works (Matt. 28:20).

Is. 1:17 says, "Learn to do good; seek justice, reprove the oppressor; defend the fatherless, plead for the widow." Before getting saved, most people lived only for themselves. But now, under the influence of God's grace, they can receive the wisdom and desire to be a blessing to others. With time and effort and much repetition they can learn to do acts of kindness that benefit those around them. Just go out and be nice to people over and over again. A disciple is a learner, an apprentice. He is not a student in a classroom so much as he is one who learns by observing and then by doing. In other words, you learn good works by doing good works. Practice makes perfect. Good works will be profitable when they are learned and maintained. You should always be ready to do good as much as you are able. You should not need to be urged, coaxed, or persuaded. Count it a privilege to have the opportunity to bless another person. Matthew Henry said, "Mere good words and good meanings are not enough without good works."

The good works you do should shine forth in a dark and hurting world. In Greek the word "good" means 'beautiful, excellent, precious, surpassing, commendable, admirable.' The more good works you do, the better this world will be. Everything that can promote the well-being of others is to be studied and performed. Learning is to take in biblical truths that causes transformation in our lives so that we become vessels that bear good fruit that lasts for eternity. Study what love is and then go out and do it. Engage in the lives of others. Provide for them some special or superior benefit. An unknown author said, "Some people are like good watches. They're pure gold, open-faced, always on time, dependable, quiet, busy, and full of good works." British theologian Donald Guthrie said, "All who engage in such works of mercy need never fear that they will be unfruitful." God doesn't want anyone to be idle. He wants all men and women to do good works so they don't end up with nothing to show for their lives."

| 14 |

"NEW FRONTIERS"

There is a popular saying that says, "Always be content but never satisfied." This is the attitude all men and women should have in their quest to impact the world. Contentment is a feeling of quiet happiness and fulfillment. It comes from having the confidence that God loves you and you're living the life He created you to live. In our quest to fulfill our destiny, we must all crawl before we walk. Zech. 4:10 says, "Do not despise these small beginnings, for the Lord rejoices to see the work begin." Consider a king being born in a manger. That seems like a small thing, doesn't it? How about that same baby growing up and proclaiming a kingdom that will change the world? The lesson here is that small things add up. Instead of despising and becoming discouraged with the small and ordinary, rejoice that God is working through you. He is weaving your small moments into a large testimony. Keep doing what you're doing. The God who multiplies loaves and fishes will multiply your faithfulness too.

Small things matter in the Kingdom of God. He takes the simple acts of obedience - the prayer no one hears, the kindness no one sees, the quiet faithfulness that never makes headlines - and He breathes His power into them. Jesus taught that the Kingdom of Heaven is like a mustard seed: tiny, unimpressive, almost invisible. Yet planted and nurtured, it becomes something strong and life-giving. In the same way, the small choices you make in faith are adding up. Every step of obedience, every moment of surrender, every small act of love becomes a seed God uses to grow something far greater than you can imagine. Don't despise the days of small beginnings. Rejoice in them. Rejoice not because they are perfect, but because God is in them. Rejoice because God has chosen to work through you, even in the small and ordinary. Rejoice because nothing done in faith is ever wasted.

Small things are ordained by a very big God. Don't despise the card you sent to encourage a shut-in or the phone call you made to check in on someone who is ill. Don't despise doing small things because they make a big difference in the lives of others. People are encouraged by what you do. Small things change hearts and impact lives. Big things start small. Jesus said the kingdom "is like a mustard seed planted in the ground. It is the smallest of all seeds, but it becomes the largest of all garden plants" (Mark 4:31,32). Small beginnings are the seeds that sow potential. In time that mustard seed "grows long branches, and birds can make nests in its shade" (vs. 32). Be content with the small things God would have you do. Vincent van Gogh said, "Great things are done by a series of small things brought together." Embrace your day of small beginnings knowing that the little things you do are ordained, seen, cherished, and blessed by God Himself.

What you do may seem small and insignificant but they're not. They are all building blocks in a quest to make this world a better place. Be content in what you're currently doing but don't be satisfied. Just like a small spark can create a huge forest fire, small things done in love can turn into big things. There is more out there for you to do but you must first be faithful in doing the small things. Luke 16:10 says, "He who is faithful in a very little thing is faithful also in much." God is looking for men and women who want to do more for Him, people who are content but not satisfied, people willing to go the extra mile and do whatever it takes to get the job done. One such man was Jabez who prayed in 1 Chron. 4:10, "Oh, that you would bless me indeed, and enlarge my territory." He wasn't asking for more real estate, He was asking God to give him more influence in the world. He was a man who was not satisfied with where he was at.

Without hesitation he addressed God with intense zeal and faith asking for a change in his life. He clearly expressed his heartfelt desire to do more for God. The most incredible part of this prayer is that "God granted him what he requested" (vs. 10). Your impact on the world can increase simply by asking God to make it happen. We often think influence comes from great talent, perfect timing, or extraordinary opportunities. But Scripture reminds us that the true source of empowerment is God Himself. When you ask God to enlarge your influence, you're inviting His strength to work through your weakness, His wisdom to guide your choices, and His favor to open doors no human effort could force open. Your simple prayer of faith can spark a ripple effect that touches lives, heals hearts, and glorifies Christ far beyond your reach. Don't underestimate what God can do with a willing heart. Ask boldly. Believe fully. Surrender completely.

God delights in using the ordinary to accomplish the extraordinary and your impact can multiply the moment you place it in His hands. The prayer of Jabez teaches us that a fervent believer in God can transform their existence by the mere act of making serious wishes made known to God. It is true that your thoughts and prayers can positively influence the course of events in this world if you really believe they will. Life is what you make it so consciously decide to be used mightily by God, relying always on vigorous faith and unrelenting tenacity. Have a burning thirst and hunger to overcome the restrictions the world may put on you and go out and achieve what you set your heart to do. When the world seems to be against you, and it will be, know with certainty that no weapon formed against you will prosper (Is. 54:17). Nothing is set in stone and with a little faith and dissatisfaction you'll find the means to rise up and believe God to enlarge your territory.

Ask God to be forever at your side. This shows you have unwavering confidence in Him as you faithfully acknowledge that every real success comes solely from Him. Nothing is impossible when you place all your faith in heavenly hands. Rom. 8:31 asks, "If God be for us, who can be against us?" Be like Jabez who had a very clear vision for his life. He knew precisely what he wanted to accomplish and he asked God to make it happen. God granted his bold request because it was authentic and came straight from his heart. He was a humble man who understood his dependence on divine support. He did not rely on his own ability to impact the world but rather on God's goodness. It is a wonderful thing that God always responds to the humble. The moment you lay down self-reliance and admit, "Lord, I need You," heaven leans in. Grace flows. Strength rises. Doors open. Battles shift. Not because of what you can do, but because of who He is. It's true, through the humble, God does His greatest work.

Jabez's fervent call shows an intense desire to honor God through his life. He asked for greater influence in the world and the responsibility that went with it. You also need to ask God to enlarge your territory because as Jesus said in Matt. 9:37, "The harvest truly is plentiful, but the laborers are few." Jabez saw opportunities for impact all around him and wanted to expand his ability to help others and to serve God's purposes. Pray daily and ask God for open doors to reach more people with a helping hand, with sound wisdom, and with a well-timed word of encouragement. Dare to pray courageously. James 5:16 says, "The effective fervent prayer of a righteous man avail much." Bold prayers open the door for God to work powerfully in your life. Jer. 33:3 says, "Call to Me, and I will answer you, and show you great and mighty things which you do not know." Seek the Lord with all your heart, trusting in His goodness and faithfulness. Pursue God's daily and rely on His presence and empowerment.

Trust God to enlarge your territory, to enlarge your capacity to make an impact in the world for His kingdom and glory. As you walk with Him many doors will be opened for you to influence other people. He'll lead you into many new adventures far beyond what you can imagine. When you seek God with your whole heart, something powerful begins to happen inside you. The more you lean into His presence, the more He shapes your desires, strengthens your steps, and aligns your life with His purpose. God never ignores a heart that sincerely reaches for Him. He lifts, He restores, and He guides. As you pursue Him with everything in you, He will raise you to new heights, to places you could never reach in your own strength. His favor begins to open doors. His wisdom begins to light your path. His love begins to overflow from your life into the lives of others. And soon, almost without realizing it, you find yourself becoming a force for good in this world.

Jabez prayed a prayer that got the attention of God. Notice that before he asked God to enlarge his territory, he first prayed for God to bless him. He said, "Oh, that you would bless me indeed." Know with certainty that God wants to bless you beyond your wildest dreams. Ps. 5:12 says, "For surely, O Lord, You bless the righteous; You surround them with Your favor as with a shield." The question that needs to be asked is, "Why does God want to bless you? Why does He want your life to overflow with His goodness and kindness?" The answer is found in what God said to Abraham back in Gen. 12:2, "I will bless you and make your name great; and you shall be a blessing." When God blesses you, it is your responsibility to do all you can to be the channel of that blessing to those around you.

Don't be selfish and only ask God to meet your needs. No, ask Him to bless you so that you can be used by Him to help meet the needs of others.

When you stop praying selfish prayers, God will do for you "exceedingly abundantly above all that you ask or think" (Eph. 3:20). The blessings of God are not just for you. They're meant to be used to make a positive impact on entire families, cities, and nations. Being blessed by God means you never have to stop and ask Him for money in order to obey Him and to what is in your heart. True prosperity is when you use what God gives you to bless others. It's not about mansions, boats, and cars. It's about influence and impact. It's about having the means to fulfill your calling, about enlarging your life so you can make a bigger impact for God and His kingdom. Pray to God and say, "Lord, give me more than I need so I can be a blessing to the world around me." Then, like with Jabez, believe that God will grant your request. Great things will happen when you pray sincerely for more territory, when you pray for more influence, more responsibility, more opportunities to make an impact for the God of Israel.

Be content but never satisfied believing you were born to do more than you're currently doing. God is in heaven waiting for you to ask for the opportunity to do so. God gets great delight when you have the desire to be mighty for Him, when you ask Him to expand your opportunities to touch more lives for Him. The boundary lines of your life will expand and get larger when you use your time, talents, and treasures to help make this world a better place. God said in Jer. 29:11, "For I know the plans that I am planning concerning you, plans for prosperity and not for harm, to give you a future and a hope. "As you walk with God, believe that His blessings are abundant and over-flowing in your life, that His great love and mercy will bring golden opportunities your way. Never hesitate to ask Him to enlarge your territory. Ps. 18:36 (AMP) says, "You enlarge the path beneath me and make my steps secure so that my feet will not slip."

Get in God's presence and believe He'll give you divine guidance in every step you take so that you will obediently walk on the path He has prepared for you. Talk to Him throughout the day. Say, "Lord, may Your kingdom come on the earth as a result of the influence You give me in the lives of others." Enlarging your territory speaks of an expansion into new frontiers, to go to places you've never gone before, to meet people you've never met before. Jabez was praying for territory into new frontiers, the frontier of new hearts. There were people in the world who needed what only Jabez could give them. The only thing in the heart of Jabez was increase, increase, increase. He wanted God to enlarge his territory and increase his influence and impact in the world. He understood something many believers overlook: influence is not about personal fame - it's about expanding the space where God can move through your life. He wanted his life to be a wider channel for God's power, love, and purpose.

Jabez knew his beginnings were small, marked by pain, but he refused to let his past define his destiny. He believed that God could expand what he placed in His hands. And that same God is still enlarging territories today. When you ask God to enlarge your territory, you are really asking Him to enlarge your heart. To stretch your compassion. To deepen your faith. To widen your reach. To open doors you couldn't open on your own. It's a bold prayer because it requires a bold willingness to step into what God gives you. Enlarged territory means greater responsibility. Greater impact. Greater spiritual authority. It means God trusts you to carry His name into places where hope is needed, where truth is missing, where broken people hunger for purpose. So pray like Jabez. Ask God to increase your influence - not for your glory, but for His. Ask Him to expand your opportunities, your vision, and your boldness. Ask Him to use your life as a vessel of kingdom impact. And as He enlarges your territory, walk in it with humility, courage, and faith.

God never intends for His people to stay where they started. Never! From the moment He calls us, He calls us forward from faith to faith, from strength to strength, from glory to glory. The God who begins a good work in us has no desire to leave it unfinished. His plan is increase, growth, maturity, expansion, and transformation. He wants all His followers to grow and increase in their love and service for Him because in the Kingdom of God, standing still is never the goal. Every season is designed to stretch us, shape us, and deepen our relationship with Him. He wants His people to rise higher in love, walk deeper in obedience, and overflow more abundantly in service. The grace He gives today is not meant to be yesterday's level of grace; it is meant to carry you into greater places of purpose. You were never meant to stay where you started. You were meant to increase in faith, in love, in devotion, and in service to the King. Let God take you further than you've ever been, and you will discover that every step forward reveals more of His goodness, more of His power, and more of His purpose for your life.

The territory of Jabez represented his life, his work, his influence. Likewise, your territory is the boundaries of everything in your life. Your territory is every place you have influence. This includes your home, your church, your workplace, your school, your social media platform. Your God-given call and all your visions and dreams are part of your territory. The boundaries of your territory is everything God has placed under your care. Be like Jabez and pray for God to increase your influence in the lives of those who are in the boundaries of your ever-increasing territory. As Jabez stepped out of his comfort zone and into the darkness of the world, he knew God's presence would be needed at all times. This is why after asking God to bless him and expand his territory, he made his third request to God, "I pray that Your hand would be with me" (1 Chron. 4:10). The hand of God's presence (Acts 11:21) is upon you and He'll give you the guidance and all the strength you need on your journey to impact the world.

God assures us in Is. 41:13, "For I, the Lord your God, will hold your right hand, saying to you, 'Fear not, I will help you.'" Throughout the Bible we see where God takes frail humanity and puts His hand on them. It was God's presence that allowed these people to do great exploits for Him. God chooses people, He puts His hand on them, and great things happen.

Your territory can only be enlarged if the hand of God's presence is on your life. This is something you need to pray for each and every day. Be like David who prayed in Ps. 51:11, "Do not cast me away from Your presence, and do not take Your Holy Spirit from me." The Message Bible says in 2 Cor. 3:6 that the hand of God's presence is "Spirit on spirit, His life on our lives!" The Greek word for "Spirit" is "pneuma" and it means 'breath.' Concerning Adam, Gen. 2;7 says God "breathed into his nostrils the breath of life." It is God's breath that puts wind in your sails. The breath of His presence will give you the confidence to boldly go where you've never gone before.

Jabez closes out his prayer with a request for divine protection, "Let Your hand be with me, and keep me from harm so that I will be free from pain" (1 Chron. 4:10). The Message Bible says, "And provide Your personal protection. Don't let evil hurt me." Ps. 3:3 says, "But You, O Lord, are a shield for me." Declare openly that you are under God's protection, believing that He will guard you from the evil schemes of the enemy. Yes, trouble will come but Rom. 8:37 says, "In all these we are more than conquerors through Him who loved us." Go to Him in faith and say, "Lord, strengthen me in the battle and rescue me from every attack of the enemy." Say to Him, "I declare that Your power is at work in me, and I believe that You can exceed all my hopes and expectations and do the impossible in my life. Lord, I pray that You will give me the courage to step out in faith and impact the world, to take bold risks for Your kingdom." Josh. 1:9 says, "Be strong and courageous. Do not be afraid, do not be discouraged, for the Lord your God will be with you wherever you go." Amen and amen!

| 15 |

"NO GREATER JOY"

The deepest desire of every man and woman should be to one day hear the Lord say to him, "Well done, good and faithful servant" (Matt. 25:23). To impact the world, you must first become what the world needs to see. You must be a faithful steward, making the most of what God has given you in this life. True influence doesn't begin with power, popularity, or position - it begins with goodness. Jesus said that a tree is known by its fruit, and in the same way, your life is known by the goodness you choose to walk in each day. When your heart is pure and your actions reflect the love of Christ, you become a light that others cannot ignore. Through works of goodness, the love of God in your heart is transferred to others. Your acts of kindness are profitable, useful, and beneficial to those around you. Every day is a chance to make the most of what God has placed in your life. Every opportunity is a doorway to obedience. Every talent is an invitation to serve. Every blessing is a platform to bless others.

Doing good is not just an act - it is a calling. God has placed you on this earth with purpose, intention, and divine opportunity. Every kind word, every honest choice, every moment you help someone who cannot repay you are seeds that heaven uses to change lives. When you choose to do good even when no one is watching, you shine with the character of Christ. To impact the world, you must be a faithful steward. God has entrusted you with time, talents, resources, and influence. None of these are accidental. They are holy tools placed in your hands to accomplish kingdom work. Stewardship is not only about managing what you have - it's about maximizing it for God's glory. When you use what He gave you with diligence, humility, and excellence, you honor the One who entrusted it to you. Your life is a message. Make it one that reflects the goodness of God. Be good. Do good. And be faithful with what He has given you because through you God can touch the world.

Dependability, discipline, and diligence are traits of a good leader. People are looking for good Christians to follow, men and women of God they'll let influence their lives. Your faithfulness will determine the responsibilities you are rewarded with in God's kingdom. If you are faithful over a few things, you'll be made ruler over many things (Matt. 25:21). A person with integrity who manifests godly character will be faithful in whatever it is God would have him or her do, whether the task be great or small. Being a faithful servant means that the most insignificant task that springs from a heart devoted to God's will has utmost importance and eternal value. A faithful believer does their best all the time. Not because people are watching, not because applause is waiting, and not because recognition might come - but because their heart is set on honoring God. Col. 3:23 says, "Whatever you do, work at it with all your heart as though you were working for the Lord rather than men."

This verse lifts our eyes above earthly approval and places our focus on the One who sees everything done in love, humility, and excellence. A faithful believer understands that every task - great or small - becomes an act of worship when it is done with a sincere heart. Folding laundry, showing kindness, leading a ministry, helping a stranger, going to work, or enduring hardship becomes sacred when your motivation is to please God. Doing your best is not about perfection - it's about devotion. It's about pouring your heart into each moment because the Lord deserves your whole heart, not half-effort or divided attention. So today, choose to give God your best. When He assigns you a certain task that will impact the world, labor at it diligently without grumbling or reluctance. Do it honestly and cheerfully. Give Him excellence in your actions, integrity in your decisions, and sincerity in your service. For when you do, heaven takes notice. And what you offer to God in faithfulness will never be wasted.

The term "working hard" describes toiling earnestly, eagerly, and tirelessly with much energy and zeal. This is a command that is to be your lifestyle and habitual practice. Everything you do for God should be characterized by an enthusiasm, confidence, and intensity not found in the attitude of the unsaved. Eccl. 9:10 says, "Whatever your hand finds to do, do it with all your might." Do everything in the name of the Lord

Jesus (Col. 3:17) to the glory of God (1 Cor. 10:31). If the world is to become a better place and if God's purposes are to be fulfilled, then we must not neglect the ordinary tasks in pursuit of the glorious ones. No service for Christ is insignificant! Your duty is to work for God's glory, and no task is better than another. Each should result in bringing honor to God. Never forget that you are doing your work unto the Lord and He expects and deserves your best effort in everything you do. Keep going for God!

We never retire from the work we've been called to do. Ps. 92:14 says, "They shall still bear fruit in old age; They shall be fresh and flourishing." A faithful man or woman is planted in the house of the Lord. They are like a tree that is full of sap and flourishing. They are a living memorial who shows that God is a faithful God. Faithful and constancy are ingredients in the obedience God requires. Age makes other things decay but makes a true child of God flourish abundantly. To impact the world you must surrender the care of your life to God. Faithfulness comes from having total confidence in God's plan, God's care, and God's guidance in your life. It will help you to be faithful when you understand the truth that God is using you and what you do for Him has eternal value even though you may not see it now. 1 Cor. 15:58 says, "Be steadfast, immovable, always abounding in the work of the Lord, knowing that your labor is not in vain in the Lord." Stand firm! Let nothing move you!

The AMP says, "Always abounding in the work of the Lord, always being superior, excelling, doing more than enough in the service of the Lord." This is more than a command - it is an invitation into a higher way of living. God never called you to a life of bare-minimum faith or half-hearted obedience. He called you to a life that excels, that overflows, that goes beyond what is required because His grace within you is more than sufficient. To abound means to exceed the limits. It means to rise above average effort, above ordinary dedication, and above casual commitment. When you abound in the work of the Lord, you don't serve Him out of duty alone - you serve out of love, passion, and a deep awareness that you are partnering with heaven itself. God empowers His people not simply to get by, but to be superior in character, excellent in spirit, and abundant in good works. Christ didn't redeem you to be stagnant, weary, or ineffective. He placed His Spirit within you so you could do more than enough - not in your own strength, but in His.

The world may settle for mediocrity, but God calls you higher. Your life becomes a testimony that He is worthy of your best. And as you abound in His work, you discover that His joy abounds in you. His strength abounds in you. His purpose abounds in you. So keep serving. Keep giving. Keep sowing. Keep loving. Not reluctantly, not minimally but abundantly. Everything you do in excellence brings glory to His name. And always be aware that your labor in the Lord is not futile. It is never wasted or nor is it without purpose. The MSG says, "Nothing you do for Him is a waste of time or effort." The future hope of one day hearing God say, "Well done, good and faithful servant" should motivate present faithfulness. It should cause you to be steadfast and immovable. The word "be" means 'to come into existence, to cause to become' (John 1:3). This is a command calling for continual attention to be given to being faithful and steadfast.

Always live with a sober sense of responsibility and accountability to the One who called you to service. Be immovable in your faith as you set out to fulfill your destiny. The end is near and you must keep steady as you move forward. Keep on going and don't let up. Put your hand to the flow and don't take it off until the work is done. Increase your efforts to serve the Lord as the great day of His return fast approaches. Be like Paul who said in 1 Cor. 15:10, "I labored even more than all of them, yet not I, but the grace of God that was with me." These words reveal the heart of a believer who understood two things deeply: the calling to work, and the source that makes that work possible. Paul did not live a casual Christian life. He threw his whole heart, soul, and strength into the mission God gave him. He pressed when tired. He prayed when weary. He preached when opposed. He endured when others quit. Paul never credited his strength, effort, or perseverance to himself. He understood that every ounce of his labor flowed from God's grace working in him. And that is the model for us.

The Greek word for "steadfast" is "hedraios" and it literally means 'firmly seated.' It refers to that which is firm, settled, steady, unshakable. A person who is steadfast is always abiding, constant, dedicated, dependable, enduring, established, faithful, firm, fixed, immovable. They are loyal, persevering, reliable, resolute, single-minded, stable, unfaltering, unflinching, unswerving, unwavering, wholehearted. The word means to be totally immobile and motionless. In God's will we are always abounding in the work of the Lord. We don't move an inch away from His will. Those who are steadfast are immovable. They're not tossed to and fro and are not moved from one place to another. Their lives are firmly anchored to the will of God. Being immovable means you remain faithful in times of trial and hardship. You don't get knocked over but always keep your balance. Stand strong and be unshaken when the rains come down and the floods come up and the winds blow and beat against your house.

Don't let the devil push you around. Be like a boulder that can't get washed away and like a tree that can't get blown over. Be like Paul who said in Acts 20:24, "But none of these things move me, nor do I count my life dear to myself, so that I may finish my race with joy." The TPT says, "I don't esteem my life as indispensable. It's more important for me to fulfill my destiny and to finish the ministry my Lord Jesus has assigned to me." This is the cry of a soul fully surrendered, fully convinced, and fully devoted to the One who called them. Paul had pressures, trials, threats, uncertainties, and enemies - yet he stood immovable. Why? Because his life wasn't anchored to comfort; it was anchored to purpose. His security wasn't in ease; it was in obedience. His joy wasn't in circumstances; it was in Christ alone. Joy is not found at the starting line. Joy is found in faithfulness. Joy is the reward of the one who refuses to be moved by fear, pressure, or distraction. Joy belongs to the one who runs with endurance, eyes fixed on Jesus, heart anchored in eternity.

A faithful man or woman who is steadfast and immovable is "always abounding in the work of the Lord." Notice the word "always." It means 'at all times.' Paul is saying there is no room for slackers in the army of the Lord. There is to be no deviation from the work God has called you to do. Children of God are called into continual, active service to the Lord, to be fruitful in the field He places us. You must be faithful at all times or else it is not faithfulness. Have a deep longing inside of you to fill the remaining years of your life aggressively impacting the world for God's glory and honor. Missionary David Brainerd said, "My soul was refreshed and comforted, and I could not but bless God who has enabled me in some good measure to be faithful in the day past. Though my body was feeble and wearied with preaching and much private conversation, yet I wanted to sit up all night and do something for God. Oh, how sweet it is to be spent and worn out for God."

Like David Brainerd, may you never loiter on your heavenly journey. The word "abounding" means 'to flow over the edges, to cause to excel a fixed amount, to overflow, to excel or to be in abundance. 'You are not only to always be serving but also to abound in service. All the men and women of God need to serve as much as they can and as often as they can. The term "always abounding" is the language of being involved in as much labor for the Lord as possible and at all times. Theologian A. W. Pink said we should "rest not satisfied with present progress and attainments, but each fresh day endeavor to perform your duty better than on the previous one." Every day strive to have the work you do for the Lord be like a river overflowing its banks. Fill your day with things that count for

Christ. Be like Jesus who said, "I must work the works of Him who sent me while it is day; the night is coming when no one can work" (John 9:4).

The Message Bible says, "We need to be energetically at work for the One who sent me here, working while the sun shines. When night falls, the workday is over." How can we take it easy and not work when so many people are spiritually dead and in need of edification, encouragement, and help of every sort? The answer is we can't. With surrendered hearts and wills we must fervently pour out ourselves, excelling in our labor for the Lord. Let us not grow weary while doing good (Gal. 6:9). 1 Thess. 3:12 says, "May the Lord cause you to increase and abound in love for one another, and for all people." MSG, "And may the Master pour on the love so it fills your lives and splashes over on everyone around you, just as it does from us to you." Working for God has eternal significance. He who does not work is not acknowledged as a servant of Christ. If he be not a servant, he is not a son. And if not a son, then not an heir. In the parable of the talents the unprofitable servant was cast into outer darkness where there will be weeping and gnashing of teeth (Matt. 25:30).

Notice that the work we do is called "the work of the Lord." It is not our work we do, it's His work and we've been invited to join Him in the work He is doing. Every born-again man and woman is called to be a workman for God. They work daily to bring glory and honor to their Master. Not only do they work for the Lord, but they also abound in that work. 1 Cor. 16:10 says, "Now if Timothy comes, see that he may be with you without fear; for he does the work of the Lord, as I also do." The "work of the Lord" is work He Himself was employed. Luke 19:10 says, "For the Son of Man came to seek and to save that which was lost." John Angell James said in the 19th century, "This was the work on which His heart was set when it beat in the babe of Bethlehem, and when it bled on the thrust of the spear." What a great honor it is to be engaged with Jesus in the work of enlightening the world, of influencing people to live better lives.

As a workman for God, you are to seek the advancement of His cause with great zeal and determination, to make His kingdom come on earth as it is in heaven. And because it's His work, He gets the glory. Ps. 115:1 says, "Not to us, O Lord, not to us, but to Your name give glory because of Your lovingkindness." Indeed, God will be glorified in the works you do, when you extend His fame throughout the earth, when you multiply the hearts that love Him and the tongues that sing His praise. You are to be a willing instrument of His power on the earth, a golden vessel used daily. Your success is His honor, and His honor is your reward. Your work for the Lord should not only be excellent in quality but plenteous in quantity. We are all commanded to always abound in the work of the Lord. If you are to always abound in this work, you must eagerly embrace every favorable opportunity for performing it. Always be mindful of the opportunities that come your way.

Imitate the conduct of Jesus who went about doing good wherever He went. Consider it an honor and a great privilege to do the work of the Lord. Do something for God every day of your life "knowing that your labor is not in vain in the Lord" (1 Cor. 15:58). In other words, working for Jesus is not an exercise in futility. Paul wants you to know beyond a shadow of a doubt that your work for the sake of the Lord is an exercise in fruitfulness that will last and last. Heb. 6:10 says, "For God is not unjust. He will not forget how hard you have worked for Him and how you have shown your love to Him by caring for other believers, as you still do." The Message Bible says, "God doesn't miss anything. He knows perfectly well all the love you've shown Him by helping needy Christians and keeping at it to the finish." Every man and woman should be fully assured that a genuine endeavor to promote God's glory will receive His smile here and His "well done good and faithful servant" hereafter.

This is why you should be patterns of Christian activity for others to follow. Push yourself to new efforts in your quest to impact the world around you. English bishop J. C. Ryle said, "Activity in doing good is one recipe for being cheerful Christians. It's like exercise to the body, and it keeps the soul in health." It has been said that "action is the very life of the soul." Always abounding in the work of the Lord is the way to keep clear and free from the pollution of the world. Take comfort knowing that life is not in vain if it is lived according to the will of God. Every good deed you do carries success within itself. Work is not done for its own sake. 1 Peter 4:11 says your aim in the work you do should be "that in all things God may be glorified through Jesus Christ." No matter how difficult or seemingly meaningless your work appears, it is meaningful to

God because it brings Him glory. For that reason, your work is not in vain.

When bringing glory to God becomes the deliberate purpose of your life, the work you do will rise to a higher level and lift you into living fellowship with your beloved Savior. Because your labor for the Lord is never worthless or futile, you can find encouragement to keep honoring and serving Him in all you do. Bible translator J. B. Phillips said, "Nothing you do for Him is ever lost or ever wasted." It's not the results that bring glory to God, it's the labor you put forth. After saying, "Well done, good and faithful servant," the master said, "Enter into the joy of the Lord." The NIV says, "Come and share your master's happiness." There is no greater joy in life than knowing you're brought happiness to the heart of Jesus because you were faithful to do what He asked you to do. The world offers many kinds of satisfaction, but none compare to the deep, quiet joy that comes from simple obedience, from doing what He asked you to do, even when no one else sees it, applauds it, or understands it.

This should be the driving force of your life, that you would make Jesus proud of the life you have lived. Every time you step out in faith, every time you choose love over anger, humility over pride, compassion over convenience, Jesus notices. He sees the moments when you say yes to Him. He sees the sacrifices no one else sees. And His heart is moved. To know that your obedience puts a smile on the face of your Savior is the highest reward. It is the kind of joy that cannot be shaken by circumstances, criticism, or fear. It's the joy of a heart aligned with heaven, of a life that reflects His love. Keep walking in faith. Keep listening when He whispers. Keep doing what He asks no matter how small it might seem. Let pleasing Him be the reason you get up each morning. When pleasing God becomes your motivation, you rise with confidence because you know your day is rooted in eternal purpose. When you do that, you delight the very heart of Jesus. And there is no greater joy than that.

| 16 |

"MARCHING ORDERS"

To be successful in your quest to make an impact in the world, you must have the same eager willingness as the prophet Isaiah. Is. 6:8 says, "Then I heard the voice of the Lord, saying, 'Whom shall I send, and who will go for us?' Then I said, "Here am I! Send me.'" Isaiah had just been cleansed from his sins (vs. 5-7) and now he is fit for holy service. He now longs to be used by God to impact the world. When it comes to being used by God, those very well may be the five most important words in all of scripture. They are simple, but they carry the weight of a surrendered life. They reflect a heart that is not negotiating with God, not offering Him conditions, not waiting for perfect circumstances - just availability, readiness, and trust. God has never looked for the most talented, the most accomplished, or the most popular. But He has always looked for the willing. Heaven leans in when a believer stands before God and says, "Use me. Take my life. Write Your story through me."

You are to embrace His calling not because you feel worthy, but because He is worthy; not because you have the strength, but because He supplies it. "Here am I! Send me" is the cry of a heart that refuses to sit on the sidelines of faith. It is the voice of someone who understands that the greatest privilege in life is not being blessed by God but being used by God. The call of God is for everyone. To every person on the planet, God is asking, "Who will go for Us?" God is speaking. The question is, are you listening? God speaks in "a still small voice" (1 Kings 19:12) and Oswald Chambers said, "Get out of your mind the idea of expecting God to come with compulsions and pleadings." God did not lay a strong compulsion on Isaiah. The prophet was in the presence of God, he overheard the call and realized there was nothing else for Him to say. Without hesitation he offered himself to be used by God without even knowing what the assignment was.

Isaiah gave his life in holy service to God. He did not discuss his call with God as did Moses (Ex. 3:11-4:14) and Jeremiah (Jer. 1:4-10). He made himself available to God to be a vessel for the Master's use. He essentially offered himself as a blank check to be filled in as God saw fit. Isaiah's prompt response reminds us of Peter and his brother Andrew. Jesus said to them "Follow Me" and "immediately they left their nets and followed Him" (Matt. 4:19,20). Unfortunately, not everyone in the Bible answered the call of God the same way Isaiah did. For instance, Jonah answered his call by saying, "I'm not going." God called Jonah to preach repentance to the wicked people of Nineveh. "But Jonah rose to flee to Tarshish from the presence of the Lord" (Jonah 1:3). Then there was Moses who God called to confront Pharaoh and bring the children of Israel out of Egypt. Moses was very reluctant to accept his call and made every excuse not to go. Eventually he said, "My Lord, please send someone else" (Ex. 4:13).

Then there was Isaiah who said, "Here I am! Send me" (Is. 6:8). He was saying, "Whatever You want, Lord, I am ready and willing to do it. Send me." Say to the Lord, "I know You want to use me to show Your love to the world. Give me eyes to see the needs of others. Give me a heart that's ready to get involved." What prompted Isaiah to be so willing to serve God? First, he saw the majesty of God. He "saw the Lord sitting on a throne, high and lifted up" (Is. 6:1). He came into the very presence of God and had a vision that changed his life dramatically. You service to God is directly proportioned to your vision of God. How you see God and your concept of Him determines how much you will love and serve Him. Seeing God for who He really is should be all the motivation you'll ever need. Isaiah saw God sitting on His throne. This told the prophet that God is in control, that He is still always working out His plan and purpose in a world that is spinning out of control.

Second, Isaiah saw the fullness of God. Is. 6:1 says, "The train of His robe filled the temple." God's presence and His glory filled the whole room. When God fills the room, there isn't room for anything else. There are moments when God steps into a place so fully, so completely, that you can sense His presence before a single word is spoken. His glory fills the whole room not as a faint feeling, not as a passing emotion, but as a holy weight that settles over everything. When God fills the room, there is no space left for fear, doubt, or distraction. Every lesser thing retreats in the light of His majesty. When you truly see God for who He is - holy, sovereign, limitless in power and love - you realize something profound: He must always be first and foremost. Not because He demands position, but because nothing else compares. Everything else is too small, too fragile, too temporary to stand beside Him. When you see God for who He is, you will understand that He must always be first and foremost.

Third, Isaiah saw the holiness of God. The angelic seraphim are before the throne saying, "Holy, holy, holy is the Lord! The whole earth is full of His glory" (Is. 6:3). When the Jews wanted to emphasize something, they used repetition. They didn't underline it, bold it, or highlight it - they repeated it. Repetition was their way of lifting a truth above every other truth, drawing the listener's heart to the weight of what was being spoken. By saying "holy, holy, holy" the seraphim are emphasizing how great God's holiness is. They are not simply repeating a word; they are reaching for language strong enough to carry the greatness of His holiness. This is the only attribute of God in all of scripture that is repeated three times. Nowhere in the Bible does it say God is "love, love, love" or "truth, truth, truth." But it does say He is "holy, holy, holy." To mention something three times in succession was to elevate it to the highest degree. They declare it three times because once is not enough and twice cannot contain it.

Fourth, Isaiah saw the power of God. Is. 6:4 gives us a vivid glimpse of the awe-inspiring power of God, "And the posts of the door were shaken by the voice of him who cried out, and the house was filled with smoke." In this moment, Isaiah experienced the overwhelming presence of the Almighty, a presence so powerful that the very foundations of the temple trembled and the air was filled with divine smoke. It was like an earthquake or an erupting volcano. The foundation of the temple shook, and Isaiah is made aware of the omnipotent power of God. This passage reminds us that God's power is both majestic and unstoppable. The shaking of the doorposts symbolizes that nothing in creation can remain unmoved by His voice - every earthly structure, every human effort, every circumstance is ultimately under His sovereign authority. The smoke filling the house represents the mysterious glory of God, a reminder that His ways and His essence are beyond human comprehension.

When Isaiah witnessed this, he was confronted not with comfort, but with reverence. He saw the holiness of God and recognized his own inadequacy. Yet, it was in that moment of fear and humility that God could call him to service. God's power does not just awe - it sanctifies, refines, and equips those who are willing to respond. Seeing all this caused Isaiah to humble himself before God in complete surrender to Him. What else could he say but, "Here I am! Send me" Isaiah's vision is a reminder that we serve a God whose presence shakes the foundations of our lives in order to build something higher within us. When we encounter God's power, it might feel overwhelming, but it is also transformative. The voice that shakes the temple posts is the same voice that can guide, purify, and empower us to live in His holiness. Let us, like Isaiah, stand in reverence before the power of God, allowing His presence to shake off what is unholy and fill us with His glory.

Interestingly, God didn't ask Isaiah to volunteer. He merely asked if there was any person who would go and Isaiah said, "I'm available. I'll go." Isaiah's quick response displays true faith in God. He knew God is sovereign and in control. He is the source of all. He is our joy and our strength. Notice that Isaiah didn't say, "God, where do you want me to go?" or "What's in it for me?" He didn't attempt to negotiate a compromise. No, God called and Isaiah answered. God commanded and Isaiah obeyed. That's the unconditional response that comes from a heart that has seen God. Isaiah's response is simple, immediate, and without reservation. He wants to go. He wants to impact the world. He wants to influence the lives of other people. God's method in building His kingdom is by using willing and obedient servants, people who will respond to the call of God on their lives. Stand up and say, "Lord, pick me! I want to talk to people about You. I want to minister to those in need. I'm ready to go. Here I am! Send me."

Through Isaiah you'll see the need to surrender your life to God. Surrender means it's no longer your life, your plans, your purposes, but His. Paul said in Gal. 2:20, "It is no longer I who live, but Christ lives in me." He's saying, "I'm here to do whatever Jesus wants me to do." When you truly know God, when you see Him for who He is, and when you are willing to serve Him completely, then the details of the calling doesn't matter. Every man and woman who calls themself a Christian is enlisted in the army of the Lord and the marching orders from our Commander-In-Chief is found in Luke 19:13, "Occupy till I come." This is a call to faithful diligence in the work He has entrusted to us. It is not a suggestion to wait idly, but an invitation to actively steward the gifts, opportunities, and responsibilities He has placed in our hands. Let those words stir you up and give you guidance as you wake up each morning with the sole purpose of making an impact in the world.

These words are found in the parable of the minas (Luke 19:11-27). This story tells how a certain nobleman explains to ten of his servants that he is going away for a while. He gives each of them a mina, which is about three months wages, and tells them that while he is gone he wants them to "occupy till I come." The Greek word for "occupy" is "pragma" and it means 'to do business, to stay busy, to carry on, to set in motion, to accomplish.' The idea of this word involves producing good results through great effort and energy. It does not mean to be casual with the task at hand. You are to work with diligence in the power of the Spirit. You work hard to please the Lord and bring Him glory with a longing and a desire for His return. What's more, the nobleman gave them what they needed to accomplish what he wanted them to do. Because of that, he expected productivity. This is God's message to each of His servants. "Occupy till I come. Stay busy and accomplish My will for your life. Serve me and finish the work I have for you."

"Occupy till I come" reminds us that the Christian life is active, purposeful, and filled with eternal significance. They give you a clear understanding of what your purpose in life is, that you're here to bear fruit for the glory of God. Do not wait for the perfect moment or the perfect condition but engage eagerly with faith, courage, and love for your labor is never in vain when it is done for Him. The nobleman said, "I am going away, and I leave you as servants in the midst of my enemies. Be loyal to me, work in my name, prove your faithfulness." When you're close to God, you'll feel as if God has great confidence in you which you must justify by faithfully doing what He asks. For sure, God calls every real man and woman to take care of His business on the earth. God expects and demands production, for all His children to go forward and enlarge His kingdom. All of us need to be occupied with the task we have each been assigned. This is a command. God is saying, "Do it now! Don't delay! Occupy till I come!"

Christ's soon return should motivate all of us to work hard for the Lord. Now is the time to report for duty. Now is the time to say, "Here I am! Send me." Occupy yourself with the work of the Lord. Take full advantage of every opportunity that comes your way. Serve God with all your heart and soul. The term "to occupy" is a military term and it means 'to take hold of territory, to hold possession of, to take control of conquered troops and land.' Occupiers don't become like the land they occupy. Instead, they strive to mold the land they occupy into the image of their mother country. Nobody is exempted from this command. If your heart is beating and there is breath in your lungs, you are commanded to occupy till He comes. Don't let your life be marked by self-centeredness, lustful daydreaming, and idle chatter. And don't wait for conditions to be perfect. God has equipped you. God has empowered you. God has positioned you. Now is your time. Do it!

1 Cor. 3:9 says you are a co-laborer with God in building lives and saving souls. In other words, you are spiritual partners with God. He considers all men and women who are faithful to Him to be His confidants and trustees. When His people are what they ought to be, they can be trusted to take care of the Father's business. Charles Spurgeon said, "If you love your Master, you will soon discover what to do for Him, and you will do it with delight." God has much confidence in you, appealing to your honor and love for Him. He knows your heart, how you rejoice to spend your whole life in service to Him. Wherever the need is greatest in the world is the place where God receives the most glory. Go to those dark places where you can bring in the largest revenue for the Master. Show God what you're made of. Doing what no one else wants to do develops in you perseverance, patience, courage, and strength of character.

Serving God is not a path for the faint of heart. It is a journey marked by relentless toil, constant discipline, and the daily surrender of self. It is a work of continuous toil and requires great discipline. It demands perseverance when the world grows weary, patience when results seem delayed, and faith when challenges press hard. Yet, those who embrace this rigorous calling are not left empty-handed. Every act of obedience, every moment of steadfast devotion, shapes them into vessels of greater purpose. And in time, God elevates them into even higher service, using their tested strength for His eternal work. True service is costly, but its rewards are beyond measure. You have not yet reached the limit of what you can do for God. Indeed, there is more to do. Step out in faith and the Lord will graciously prosper your endeavors. Jesus is coming soon and you must continue to work hard until He does. Never are you to retire or slack off from going about doing the Father's business. Your rest will come when He returns, but until then you must work on.

You are here for one purpose and one purpose only. You're here to live for Christ, to seek first the expansion of His kingdom on the earth (Matt. 6:33). The phrase "to live is Christ" should be the central theme of every Christ man and woman's life. Everything you say and do should point to Him. The singular aim of everything Paul tried to be, everything he became, and everything he looked forward to pointed to Jesus. From the time of Paul's conversion until his martyrdom, every move he made was aimed at advancing the knowledge, the gospel, and the church of Christ. "To live is Christ" means you work diligently to bring glory to the King of kings and Lord of lords. This is your motive as you strive to impact the world you live in. "To live is Christ" means you imitate the example of Jesus. Everything Jesus did and said is what you should do and say. Paul said, "Imitate me as I imitate Christ" (1 Cor. 11:1).

"To live is Christ" means that we are willing to give up anything and everything that prevents you from making a positive impact in the lives of others. "To live is Christ" means He is your main focus, your foremost goal, and your chief desire. He is the center point of your heart, soul, mind, and body. Paul said in Phil. 1:20, "It is my eager expectation and hope that I will not be ashamed, but that with full courage now as always Christ will be honored. "Christ is your life, our "all in all" (1

Cor. 15:28). Everything you do, you do for Christ's glory. As you run your race, lay aside every weight and fix your eyes on Jesus (Heb. 12:1,2). To impact the world you must always fix your eyes on Jesus. Heb. 12:2 (MSG) says, "Keep your eyes on Jesus, who both began and finished this race we are in." You must have vertical vision in your horizontal race. Always keep your gaze fixed on Jesus for He is your supreme example and the inspiration of your faith. Looking to Jesus is the secret to spiritual success.

Richard Phillips said in his Bible commentary that Jesus "is the source and fountain of all our spiritual vigor." Look away from all that would distract you and give Him your undivided attention each and every day of your life. Racehorses often have blinders on their eyes to keep them from looking to the sides and being distracted from their main job which is to trot on straight ahead. Like those horses you need to fix your eyes on Jesus and look straight ahead. Keep focused on what's in front of you. Pay attention to the fulfillment of your destiny. The world needs you and you can't let the devil distract you with other things. Realize that every trial you face is merely a distraction from the enemy to slow you down. This is why you must concentrate on Jesus and what He's called you to do. Have eyes for no one but Jesus. Do that and it won't be long before you'll be on your way to making this world a better place. Remember, that's what you're here for. God needs you; the world needs you; we all need you. If you'll fix your eyes on Jesus, for sure you won't let us down.

SUMMARY

As we come to the close of this book, the call of God upon our lives becomes unmistakably clear: we are not placed on this earth merely to exist, but to influence, transform, and illuminate the world around us. Jesus declared that we are the salt of the earth and the light of the world - not hidden, not silent, but active agents of change reflecting the character and love of our Father. Every believer has been entrusted with a divine assignment to make a difference right where they are.

The world is in desperate need of people who will rise above complacency and live with eternal purpose - people who will let their faith shape their actions, their compassion shape their relationships, and their hope shape the culture around them. Making an impact is not about fame, wealth, or recognition; it's about faithfulness to God's call and obedience to His Word in everyday life. It's about choosing love over apathy, righteousness over compromise, and service over self-interest.

Your impact may not always be seen or celebrated by others, but heaven takes notice. Every act of kindness, every word of encouragement, every prayer offered in faith carries eternal weight. The ripple effect of a Christ-centered life extends farther than we could ever imagine.

So go forth with confidence and conviction. Let your light shine brightly in dark places. Be bold in your faith, steadfast in your purpose, and compassionate in your service. Remember, you are God's ambassador. You are His hands, His voice, and His heart in this world. If even one life is touched, one soul is saved, or one heart is drawn closer to Christ through your obedience, your impact has been eternal.

Now is the time to live intentionally, to make your mark for the Kingdom of God, and to leave behind a legacy of faith, love, and righteousness that will echo through generations to come.